The Scoutmaster

The Scoutmaster

by Jim Boeger

Pray Publishing
St. Louis, Missouri

Fourth Printing, 1983

Copyright © 1978 by Church Commission for
Civic Youth Serving Agency

All rights reserved. No part of this book may be reproduced by any method without the publisher's permission, except by a reviewer who wishes to quote brief passages in connection with a review written for inclusion in a magazine, newspaper, or broadcast. For other permission, address: Pray Publishing, P.O. Box 6900, St. Louis, Missouri 63123.

Cover by Roger Siebe
Text Design by Roger Lattner

Library of Congress Cataloging in Publication Data

Boeger, Jim.
    The Scoutmaster.

    1. Scouts and scouting. 2. Boy Scouts.
I. Title.
HS313.B63   369.43   77-15033
ISBN 0-8272-3415-5

Distributed in Canada by The G. R. Welch Company, Ltd., Toronto, Ontario, Canada

Printed in the United States of America

Dedication

"A hundred years from now it will not matter what my bank account was, the sort of house I lived in, or the kind of car I drove. But the world may be different because I was important in the life of a boy."

This book is dedicated to those Scouters who truly believe in the above anonymous quotation.

Acknowledgments

I would like to express my sincere gratitude to all of those people who have given me an enjoyable ten years of Scouting experience.

Special thanks go to my wife, Phyllis, who had enough sense to let me do my thing and didn't tie a couple of apron strings around my waist; to my parents who gave me a firm foundation on which to build; to my mother for her help in editing and typing this manuscript; to my Scouts for being boys; to their parents for loaning their sons to me, sometimes for weeks at a time; and to my many fellow Scouters across the country for the enjoyable times, campfires, and trails we have shared together.

Table of Contents

		page
Foreword.		9
Preface.		10
Chapter 1	Getting Started	11
Chapter 2	Kids Will Be Kids	17
Chapter 3	The Scouting Program	29
Chapter 4	Scouting Builds Character	35
Chapter 5	Why Bother?	45
Chapter 6	Heartbreak Hill	51
Chapter 7	Close Calls	58
Chapter 8	Accepted As Something Special.	63
Chapter 9	High Adventure	71
Chapter 10	The Future	108
Biographical Sketch.		112

Foreword

Chapter 3 begins simply by stating, "There is nothing magic about the Scouting program." I would agree, as the magic is when men like our author make the program live in the lives of youth.

Jim Boeger is a relatively young man to be able to look back, as he does, in his book *The Scoutmaster* on so many Scouting adventures. In addition, Scouting came late to our author. You find him being thrust into Scouting, (as so many of us have) by a friend who needed help for a Scouting activity. Scouting quickly claimed our author as its own. Like flint and steel, Scouting and our author seem made for each other.

Since the beginning of the century there have been many Jim Boegers. Such men have made Scouting great. More important, however, is the fact that such men have made a difference for millions of boys (many now men) who have come under the Scouting banner.

As a movement, Scouting is indebted to men like Jim Boeger. Think back, if you will, to your Scoutmaster and dream awhile. Let the smell of the campfire once again fill your being. Forget the cares of adulthood for the moment and be a boy again.

Van R. Braidwood
Scout Executive
Saukee Area Council
Boy Scouts of America

Preface

New challenges are what seem to make life worthwhile. Any new adventure is usually great the first time, pretty good the second time, but the edge of excitement can soon wear off. We must continually give ourselves new challenges, new mountains to climb, new rivers to cross, if we are to continue to grow as an individual.

Writing this book is my latest challenge. I do not pretend to be a great author nor do I intend to write a second book. If you expect a great novel, you are going to be disappointed. If you expect a deep plot, you are going to be disappointed. What you will find in this book is a recalling of many true incidents that have happened to me as Scoutmaster over the past several years. Mixed in is a little humor, some homespun philosophy, a few needles poked at parents who don't care enough, and a sales pitch on the program of the Boy Scouts of America.

Scouting has indeed been good to me over the years. It has often been said that one receives in direct proportion to what he gives. From my vantage point, whatever I have given to Scouting has been returned tenfold in terms of self-satisfaction.

My purposes in writing this book are threefold:

1. Hopefully it will allow other Scoutmasters to recall and enjoy fond memories of trails that were steep, campfires that were warm, and campsites that were perhaps muddy or rocky.

2. Perhaps it will serve as an inspiration to the new Scout leader who isn't really sure if it is all worth it; or to the person just looking for a place where he is needed and can get involved.

3. And finally, the writing of this book gives me a great excuse to put off until tomorrow all of those "honey do" chores that are waiting around the house.

Clyde Kangas

Chapter 1

Getting Started

Someone once said that the easiest way to hike from San Francisco to New York is to do it one step at a time. Undoubtedly the first step is the hardest, which is usually the case in making the decision to become a Scout leader. There are always a million excuses why we don't have time; don't know how, can't stand kids, don't have a tent, usually develop a sore toe every Wednesday night, etc., etc.

For me, getting started in Scouting came quite easily and unintentionally. After graduating from Purdue University in 1965, I became employed in Grand Haven, Michigan, with Gardner-Denver Company. Being single and loving the out-of-doors, I readily found friends who liked camping, hunting, fishing, and boating.

One week early in January, Bill McCartney asked me if I wanted to go along with him for the weekend to a cabin on Lake Michigan just south of town. Not having a date, it sounded better than staying home and cleaning the apartment, so I readily accepted.

When I turned on to Pennoyer Street after work that Friday evening, there was a beehive of activity around his house. At first I thought there had been a fire or car wreck, but not seeing any flashing red lights soon ruled that out. The thought never occurred to me that I had been conned into a program that would give me pleasure the rest of my life, You guessed it. Bill McCartney was Scoutmaster of Troop 5 sponsored by the United Methodist Church of the Dunes in Grand Haven, and "our troop" was going camping for the weekend.

It seemed like kids were running everywhere with worried mothers calling last minute instructions to their cherubs, which of course were falling on deaf ears. Being new, I was totally ignored in the confusion of getting cars packed with gear. Bill appeared to be Mr. Calm and Cool in spite of four kids asking him questions all at once, and then running off to do their thing without waiting for an answer. One big kid, who I later learned was Senior Patrol Leader Karl Whiteman, pointed to my car and said, "Load it up," and before I could utter a sound, it was filled floorboard to ceiling with sleeping bags, packs, and kids.

Not even knowing who these strangers in my car were, nor where we were going, I was soon following Scoutmaster Bill's taillights south on Lake Shore Drive.

One point did make an impression in me. Most parents would never even consider letting their sons get into a car with a complete stranger and take off for the weekend, yet they all had complete trust and confidence in their Scoutmaster to bring their most precious possessions, their sons, back safe and sound at the end of the weekend. That level of responsibility scared me a little that night as I was driving south on Lake Shore Drive on my first Scouting overnight, and it scares me even more today.

What appeared to be mass confusion and chaos on the surface soon had the food put away, bed rolls on the bunks, wood cut, and a fire going in the fireplace of our cabin. We were staying in McCarthy Cabin at Camp Kirk, then owned by the Grand Valley Council—Boy Scouts of America. The cabin was of frame construction with a long table down the middle. There were wooden bunks along each wall. Heat was provided by a big stone fireplace at one end of the room and a pot-bellied stove at the other. It was rustic to say the least. The cabin was nestled in pine trees with only a lone sand dune separating it from Lake Michigan. There was a stiff January wind blowing in from the lake. Standing on the sand dune, one could hear the roar of the waves crashing into the beach and could just make out the white of the water. The sound of the waves made it seem even colder than it really was. It was just starting to snow.

After we enjoyed a generous supply of buttered popcorn, it was time to hit the sack. It was then that I made the painful discovery that my 6'9" frame would not fit into a 6'2" bunk. The long table in the middle of the room was pressed into service as a makeshift bunk, thus solving the problem.

Morning found the fires burned out, the wood supply low, and three inches of new snow on the ground outside. The boys were scurrying around getting wood, goofing off, and rummaging through the groceries to see what was for breakfast. I couldn't understand why Bill wasn't getting out of his sleeping bag and organizing the seemingly uncoordinated effort. Soon a fire was going and the boys had the cocoa mix measured into the milk to make hot chocolate. The next thing they found in the grocery box was pancake mix. All was going well until they came to the part that read "add three cups of milk." "Where's the milk?" "We used it all to make the hot chocolate." "Oh no!" "Then use some hot chocolate instead." The next few lines of instructions on the box were followed without a hitch, but then they came to the part that read "grease the skillet before adding the batter." "Where's the butter?" "We put it all on the popcorn last night." "Oh no!"

By this time Scoutmaster Bill had progressed to sitting on the edge of the bunk with one sock on and one off, wearing a smile of amused satisfaction. I must have been wearing the look of hungry frustration. It was a couple of years before I fully realized that Bill's use of the technique of controlled failure was a very effective teaching tool.

After a hearty breakfast of chocolate scrambled pancakes, the rest of the weekend went without a hitch. I enjoyed being with the kids, and they seemed to accept me as just another one of the adult leaders. So it was that I signed up the following Monday night as a member of the Troop 5 committee.

For the next several years I remained a troop committee member, interested primarily in the weekend campouts. I managed to attend most of the campouts and even made it to a few of the troop meetings, but wasn't totally involved as a fully dedicated leader.

One warm Sunday afternoon in June, I was driving home from Stearns Bayou after fishing (without much luck). It had been a nice day to be out on the water, even if the fish weren't biting. I was in no particular hurry to get home. Suddenly behind me I heard the squeal of tires. I looked in the mirror in time to see a convertible fail to make a turn, hit some loose gravel, and cartwheel end for end landing upside down. As if on instant replay, I realized there was more than one person in the car, but was not sure how many.

13

In the process of growing up on a farm, I had learned how to plow a field from dawn to dusk, how to milk a cow, how to herd cattle, how to hunt a rabbit. In school I had learned how to solve a differential equation, how to recite the Preamble to the Constitution, how to calculate a linear regression analysis. But somewhere along the line I had completely failed to learn how to handle an emergency situation. For the first time I realized that I didn't know what to do. I tried to run back to the overturned convertible but my feet felt like they were made of lead. Surely no one could be alive under that car! The tires were still spinning, the engine was racing, and there was steam coming from the radiator. I really wanted to help but didn't know what to do first.

Just then Emil Teska, a fellow employee at Gardner-Denver, came running out of his nearby home. Emil, I knew, had been a long-time Scout leader in Grand Haven. He immediately took complete charge of the situation. Other cars were stopping to help, and Emil forced others to stop until he had enough manpower to lift the car. He barked orders with authority, and every person there followed his instructions without question. What was different about this man that enabled him, within minutes, to assemble and organize about twenty-five men, complete strangers, into a team capable of lifting this overturned convertible?

I remember as though it were yesterday that I was lifting on the left rear bumper, with gasoline dripping out of the tank beside me. On Emil's command the car was lifted, and he instinctively crawled under to help whomever was still under the wreckage, knowing full well that his hastily organized team could drop the car, or it could burst into flames at any moment.

Out came two men in their mid twenties, followed by two very scared but unhurt young children, followed by many empty beer cans. By some miracle scratches and bruises were the only injuries.

Later that evening while reflecting back on the day's events, I realized that every boy should be given the opportunity to learn how to handle an emergency situation such as had occurred earlier in the day. Many parents could not impart such knowledge to their children. School programs typically do not include such training. From my halfhearted exposure to the Scouting program, I am sure that it does teach boys the fundamentals of first aid, and that every effort is made to allow Scouts to develop their leadership capabilities. It was right then and there that I decided to shift my involvement in Scouting out of low gear. For that decision, I have never been sorry.

On several occasions, men have asked me whether I thought they should become Scout leaders. Of course, I cannot answer that question for them. I believe that they really wanted me to talk them into what they had already decided to do on their own. I guess the following letter best sums up my response to the person who is on the fence as to whether he should become involved in Scouting, or any other youth program, for that matter.

I was glad to hear that you are giving serious consideration to becoming a Scout leader. Good men are badly needed. Naturally, I can't make that decision for you, but perhaps I can tell you why I am a Scoutmaster, and what some of the rewards of the job are.

To the general public and the casual observer, a Boy Scout is associated with camping, cooking, and a kid in a green uniform helping a little old lady across the street. To the trained Scoutmaster, the entire Scouting program has the aims of character development, citizenship development, and the development of physical and mental fitness. The tools of camping, cooking, the uniform, the advancement program, plus others, are all just means for achieving the three basic aims of Scouting listed above.

It is my personal opinion that the program of the Boy Scouts of America is the best tool for developing character, citizenship, and fitness, that exists in the free world today.

Before saying yes in response to being asked to assume the position of Scoutmaster, picture yourself on a hike with soaking wet boots and five miles yet to go; picture yourself eating a burnt hot dog when you know there is a steak at home in the refrigerator; picture yourself sleeping on the cold, hard ground when you have a nice bed at home. If you are considering being Scoutmaster for the publicity, or because it would look good on a job resume, forget it. If you are considering it because you feel obligated to "take your turn," do everybody a favor and say no. But if you have a genuine desire to help boys, then all of the hardships that Mother Nature can throw at you won't be able to dampen your spirit for the Scouting program.

The rewards for being Scoutmaster are tremendous. The recognition plaques, the thanks from a parent or Scout, the picture in the paper once in a while are all nice, but the real reward is watching a young mischievous kid grow into a responsible, Christian adult, and thinking that maybe, just maybe, you were able to play some small role in helping that happen.

Please stop by the house any evening if you would like to discuss further your opportunities as a volunteer Scouter.

Chapter 2

Kids Will Be Kids

Any Scoutmaster who is not able to maintain his sense of humor will surely end up on his way to the funny farm in a strait jacket. The humorous incidents that always seem to happen when kids are around add just enough spice to a campout to make it enjoyable.

Certainly all Scoutmasters have had their share of clowns, born leaders, clumsy try hards, con artists, goof-offs, etc. These characteristics seem to be the same the world over, with only the names changed from troop to troop.

For instance, I remember the Friday afternoon at the Ottawa-Chippewa Districts Camporee that was held near the consumers Power Company plant a few miles south of Grand Haven, Michigan. We just about had camp set up when suddenly I heard a new tenderfoot Scout yelling, at the top of his lungs, from the far end of the campsite, "Mr. Boeger! Mr. Boeger!" He was running my direction under a full head of steam. Of course, all of the worst possibilities crossed my mind. Was there a fire out of control in camp? Had someone been injured? Was someone lost? Halfway across the campsite our newest Scout tripped over the shovel and sprawled headfirst into the dust. All in the same movement he regained his feet and resumed his beeline in my direction. He came to a screeching halt in front of me, stirring up a cloud of dust in the process. Completely out of breath he gasped, "Mr. Boeger, have you seen the shovel? I can't find it anywhere." Who was it that said, "These are the times that try men's souls"?

Fond memories of the camporee when Albert was our guest will never be forgotten by those in attendance on that particular weekend.

It was about 3:00 P.M. on an April Friday afternoon preceding the Blackhawk District Spring Camporee to be held at Saukenauk Scout Reservation north of Quincy, Illinois. The phone rang in my office, and it was Chuck Mills, the District Scout Executive. After exchanging the usual pleasantries, I knew he wanted a favor.

Chuck related a sad tale of woe about a young Scout who had just purchased a new sleeping bag in anticipation of this camporee, and now at the last minute his Scoutmaster had cancelled the campout because not enough boys were going. Of course Chuck wondered if the young Scout could go along with Troop 9.

As I was saying "yes," Chuck interrupted saying that there was a little problem, namely that the boy was black. That didn't pose any problem, so again I was saying "yes" when Chuck again interrupted with another little problem. The boy was also hyperactive. That still didn't sound like too much of a problem to me, so young Albert was invited to join our troop for the weekend. After all, how much mischief can one 11 year old get into in just one weekend?

About an hour later Albert showed up right on time at the Vermont Street United Methodist Church. He was all decked out in a new Scout uniform, was proud as punch of his new sleeping bag, and had a sheath knife hanging from his belt that extended almost to his knees. His shirttail was out before the cars got out of the parking lot.

We were able to put some of Albert's excess energy to good use lugging equipment from the parking lot to the campsite. Albert was assigned to tent with John Fletcher, a regular Scout in our troop who also happened to be black. It soon became apparent that that arrangement wasn't going to work out at all. Albert was reassigned to tent with Fred Cory, the patrol leader for the patrol to which Albert had been assigned for the weekend. That also didn't seem to be working out, so I suggested that Albert tent with me for the night. He reluctantly agreed.

While supper was cooking that evening, I heard a commotion over in the next site where Troop 56 was camped. Then here came Albert running our direction with three big Troop 56 boys hot on his tail. It seemed that Albert got tired of waiting for our troop to cook supper, so had gone in search of food that was already prepared. The golden opportunity came when one of the Troop 56 Scouts set his hamburger down to open a can of soda. Quick as a flash Albert requisitioned the hamburger and fled in high gear. A little fast talking and the promise of three pieces of peach cobbler settled things down for the time being.

Things were calm while the plates were full, that is until the wind shifted and blew a cloud of smoke in Albert's direction. When the smoke surrounded him, he whipped out that big old sheath knife and started swinging at the smoke for all he was worth. Fortunately the only thing that got stabbed was the cloud of smoke. The knife was politely confiscated for the remainder of the camporee.

The boys were really trying to help Albert the next day during the competitive events, which everyone seemed to enjoy. But when it came time to cook lunch, his patrol thought it best not to trust Albert with the cooking. Not being bashful, nor wanting to shirk his responsibilities, Albert insisted that he be allowed to help with the cooking. Finally Senior Patrol Leader Joe Dulin compromised, and gave Albert an old pot, some French fries, and a hunk of hamburger, instructing him that he could cook his own lunch, but not to mess up anybody else's.

Joe had the troop in pretty good shape, and was really proud of the appearance of the campsite. He thought things were all ready for the judges when they made their inspection rounds. Suddenly there was a howl from the corner of the campsite where Albert had been doing his thing. There was Albert's lunch, potatoes, hamburger, pot, and all, flaming away, with Albert trying to put it out by beating on the whole mess with a stick. Out of the corner of his eye, Joe spied the judges coming down the trail toward our campsite. He sent one Scout up the trail to stall the judges and headed in Albert's direction carrying the shovel. For a second I wasn't sure if Joe was going to put the fire or Albert out with the shovel, but much to my relief he headed for the fire. He stashed the charred remains in the latrine, until after the judges had left, and then calmly proceeded to give Albert a lesson in the proper technique to be used in the preparation of a hamburger.

That night the district camping committee had arranged a pie eating contest. There was no question about it. Albert had to be the representative from our troop. The Scouts thought it would be great, but all I could think of was how I was going to explain to his Dad the lemon creme pie all over the new uniform. The contest was enjoyed by all, and the mess was as predicted.

That night about 3:00 A.M., Albert let out a scream like a wounded banshee and went charging out of my tent like his tail was on fire. It must have been a bad dream, for he woke up about the time he got to the middle of the campsite, looked around, walked back to the tent, crawled into his sleeping bag, and went back to sleep. The only problem was that he didn't wait to open the mosquito netting before going through it. Such are the breaks I guess.

Things went smoothly until I noticed a bulge under Albert's shirt just as we were getting into the cars to go home after church on Sunday morning. Investigation yielded a big bull frog. Albert was proud as he could be that he had traded some kid his new flashlight for the frog. It took me another 45 minutes to locate the flashlight and get the business deal reversed.

We didn't see Albert again, but certainly enjoy recalling that eventful camporee. I hope that Albert enjoyed the weekend as much as we enjoy the memories of it.

It seems typical that the older Scouts often try to pull rank on the newer Scouts, giving them the dirty jobs to be done around camp. Such was the case one brisk November morning at Deer Ridge Public Use Area in Lewis County, Missouri.

I was busy staying warm in my sleeping bag until the patrols had breakfast well underway—a trick I learned a few years earlier from Bill McCartney. Two patrols were getting things going in good shape, but I could hear the older Scouts of the Buckskin Patrol yelling at one of the younger Scouts to get the fire going. A lot of yelling could be heard, but the clang of pots and pans was obviously absent. Soon I rolled out of the tent to the smell of bacon and eggs coming from the Eagle Patrol campsite, the smell of pancakes coming from the Condor Patrol, and a lot of hot air coming from the Buckskins. Investigation showed the older Buckskins still in their sleeping bags barking orders at young Mike Leffman, who was holding his twenty seventh match under a four inch diameter green log, and not understanding why the fire wouldn't start.

The patrol method does work, and works very well, but on that particular morning the patrol method needed a little assistance from the Scoutmaster to get it into gear. You can rest assured that the Buckskins had their lunch prepared in record time that noon.

And then there was the time when Ben Morrison was on his first campout. Just as his patrol was sitting down for the evening meal, Ben's patrol leader pointed to the pail full of water for doing the dishes, and asked Ben to put it on the fire. Ben did. He poured the whole bucket right over the fire.

The Saukee Area Council has a group which calls itself the

Campmaster Corps. The members of the Campmaster Corps take turns spending the weekend at the local Scout Reservation. Their purpose is to assist troops with their weekend activities, handle any emergencies that may arise, and see that the rules and regulations of the reservation are adhered to. A heated cabin is made available for the Campmasters' use each weekend.

Campmasters are permitted to take three older Scouts with them for assistance with their duties on the weekends. Personally I look forward to the weekends when it is my turn to be Campmaster. It provides the opportunity to be with Scouts and Scouters, and still enjoy the comforts and conveniences of home; provides relief from television, radio, and newspapers; and most importantly, allows me to work closely with three Scouts apart from the troop environment for a whole weekend.

Don't let anyone tell you that good training can make an effective leader out of any Scout. I just don't believe that it is that easy. In my years of being Scoutmaster, I have had only six Scouts that, in my opinion, were excellent, effective leaders.

Chris Cook, Dave Botts, and Joe Dulin were such leaders. They were all three the same age in the same Troop at the same time. It was indeed a challenge for me to provide enough challenge to each of them to keep them interested and growing in the Scouting program.

One December weekend it was my turn to be Campmaster at Saukenauk Scout Reservation. These three Scouts accompanied me for the weekend. Attempting to bottle up that much energy in a cabin for a whole weekend was a feat that even Charles Atlas would have had trouble handling, I believe.

Chris and Joe decided that they would fill Dave's new rubber boots with water, and set them outside the cabin to freeze into solid chunks of ice by morning. Chris managed to keep Dave occupied while Joe filled the boots and sneaked out the door with them. Chris followed Joe out the door to help hoist the water filled boots to the top of the flagpole.

Dave, not being as naive as he pretended, locked both doors to the cabin. When the two pranksters were knocking at the window for someone to let them back in, Dave collected all of Chris' and Joe's shoes and boots, put them in the sink, plugged the drain, turned the water on, and retired to read a book on his bunk. Joe and Chris watched helplessly through the window as the sink filled with water.

Had it been any boys other than these particular three, I am sure that I would have laid down the law much sooner, but these three deserved each other. Bedlam reigned most of the rest of the evening.

When morning came, the only thing found outside filled with water, and frozen into a solid chunk of ice was a pair of my gloves. Dave thought they belonged to Chris. Chris thought they belonged to Joe. Joe thought they belonged to Dave. A couple weeks later I found a nice new pair of gloves under the Christmas tree, from my three musketeers. I am not sure whether the gift was prompted by the spirit of Christian love or the spirit of self preservation.

One never remembers the times when it didn't rain, when the sun shined all week at summer camp, or when the trail hike seemed shorter than the expected 14 miles. The memories that are branded in our brain forever are the times when things were rough and miserable; the times when we did or experienced the unusual; the times that were just a little frightening.

So it was on another spring camporee! The weather had been beautiful all weekend, and the boys were really doing a great job of carrying out their assigned responsibilities. Late Saturday afternoon the temperature suddenly dropped about ten degrees from a mild 75°. A big, black storm cloud appeared out of nowhere, and the wind started to blow. The rain started all at once like it was being poured from a bucket. The lightning crashed all around; the roar of thunder was almost continuous.

The evening meal was just finished. Our boys were scattered all over the reservation enjoying some free time. Only about half of the troop was in camp when the storm hit.

We attempted to close the flaps on a couple of the tents, but to no avail. The wind was blowing the rain right under the flaps. We hurriedly took shelter in the nearest structure, which happened to be the latrine. The rain turned to hail. One could hardly see across the campsite. The sound of hail hitting the tin roof of the latrine was ear splitting.

Then it stopped as suddenly as it had started. Our campsite looked like a disaster area. Two tents had been blown down, a third, which had been in a low spot, was now sitting in six inches of water, and a fourth had a little stream running right through the middle of it. An air mattress had floated out the back end of the tent and was snagged on some brush. Our dining fly had developed a low spot, and the weight of the water that it collected, caused the whole thing to collapse. The latrine pit had filled with water and was overflowing. Our fearless senior patrol leader and one of his assistants were stranded on the boxes of the two-holer, yelling for someone to float them a life raft. The hail was about two inches deep on the ground, with the temperature now in the low 60's. One by one our Scouts straggled back into camp, each excitedly telling of his experiences during the past half hour. A couple had knots on their heads from being pelted by large hail stones, but there were no serious injuries.

There was about half an hour of daylight left, and it was obvious that we were in no shape to spend the night. It was quickly decided to leave the troop equipment where it was until the next day, but to get the personal gear collected and into the cars before the next storm hit, which could happen anytime from the appearance of the sky. Some of the gear was a sorry looking sight.

It had been Greg Ogle's first campout, and by now he was cold, wet, and beginning to get a little scared. He had been down by the waterfront when the storm hit, so was soaked to the bone. The only dry thing that I had left was a pair of socks and tennis shoes that were in the bottom of my pack. To keep Greg from the edge of panic, I told him to go into my tent and put on the dry tennis shoes. I hoped that would at least keep him occupied long enough for me to help the older Scouts get some of the gear up to the parking lot.

The road to the parking lot was on high ground, but the shortest route from our campsite to the cars was through the archery field, which was under several inches of water, and had at least an inch of hail floating on top. We chose the longer and drier route to maneuver our gear to the cars. All went well until returning from our first trip to the cars, when we found Greg, bawling his head off, stuck in the mud in the middle of the flooded archery field, and knee deep in that icy water. He had decided to take a short cut. When we waded in to pull him out, sure enough, he was wearing my size 17 tennis shoes. They looked more like water skis on him.

With Greg rescued from the archery field, and our senior patrol leader rescued off the latrine box, all we had left to do was to get the car out of the muddy parking lot. It took the Camp Ranger and his tractor another half hour to accomplish that task.

We felt a little foolish when we got back to Quincy, for in town it hadn't rained a drop, and the skies had been clear all evening. That was one camporee that our Scouts will not soon forget.

Taking a new Scout on his first hike or campout is always a treat. They are usually so filled with enthusiasm that it seems like they are going to bubble over. Invariably questions come a mile-a-minute. The campers can usually be separated from the non-campers the first few minutes.

Larry was obviously a non-camper. He started out with a

canteen filled with bug juice (Kool Aid). After hiking a couple of miles, Larry was continually looking around. He would stand first on one foot, and then on the other. It almost looked like he was practicing for a tap dance. The problem was obvious, and soon Larry was tugging on my sleeve with, "Mr. Boeger, where is the bathroom?" It took a real sales pitch to convince him that any tree would serve the function, for there just weren't many flush facilities out in the woods. When it was time to cook our foil dinners in the coals of a campfire, it was equally hard to convince Larry that it would be all right, just this once, to eat lunch without going home to wash his hands first. What a crying shame that right here in the United States of America, a father could go 11 whole years without ever taking his son for a walk in the woods. Unbelievable! Humorous? Yes, in a sad sort of way, but also unbelievable.

There is something magnetic about a campfire that makes me want to just sit in front of it and stare into space after the rest of the crew has retired for the night. One of my favorite evening activities is telling stories around the campfire.

One of my favorite stories was a blood and guts horror tale about a giant three-legged raccoon. It seemed as if that story was requested every time a new Scout joined the troop and was on his first campout.

One particular night at Gerber Scout Reservation in Michigan, I ended the story with "and it happened right about there," pointing to the tent of our newest Scout. He said nothing, but looked a little worried. Later while we were fixing some popcorn, I noticed that Jimmy and his tent-mate were not with the group. A quick look around found them busy removing their gear from their tent and taking it down. There was no way on earth that any of us could talk them into leaving their tent in that particular spot. The tent was moved over next to mine, and things were all right for the rest of the weekend.

There is an old Civil War graveyard near my parents' farm in Missouri. It is now a cow pasture, grown up with trees and brambles. It has not been maintained for years. It is a great place to visit at night whenever we are camping in the vicinity.

One particular night was especially dark and spooky. There was a heavy cloud cover, and the wind was whistling through the red cedar trees. Assistant Scoutmaster Bill Rummenie and I led the way over hill and dale, taking the great circle route to make sure the boys were thoroughly lost by the time we arrived at the graveyard. An owl in an overhead tree, and our flashlights picking up only the eyes of a couple head of cattle, set the stage for an especially spooky experience.

Soon the boys were all occupied reading fallen tombstones and searching for others in the underbrush. They were too busy to notice Bill and me backing away from them toward a nearby ridge.

We dropped to the ground, our clothes blending in perfectly with the fallen leaves. Then one of the boys noticed that we were no longer in sight. Suddenly the field of flashlights converged into one compact circle that probably could have been covered by a silver dollar. I am surprised that the kid in the middle didn't suffocate. Flashlight beams were being swung in every direction. From our vantage point it looked like one of those old World War II movies when the searchlights are seeking out the enemy bombers overhead. Even the treetops were being scanned, for what I am still not sure.

First it got very still, and then they all started talking at once. After much discussion, they decided to stay together——very close together——and move in our direction. Closer and closer they came, all speculating as to where we were hiding. They almost stepped on Bill, stopping with one Scout's foot less than six inches from his head. Still they didn't see us, for they were too busy shining flashlights in all other directions. It was a good thing that none of them had a weak heart, for when Bill reached out and grabbed one by the leg, I thought we might have to get a hook and ladder truck to get some Scouts out of nearby trees. I believe that our heels were stepped on a dozen times that night on the way back to camp.

Troop 9 Scouts soon learned that the old saying "misery loves company" is true, but not true enough to be used as an excuse to wake up this old Scoutmaster. Emergencies or illness are legitimate reasons to rouse the Scoutmaster at any hour, but just being cold usually doesn't carry much weight. Invariably Scouts on their first Polar Bear campout will make some mistake that will result in their being cold before morning.

Don't ever think that kids are dummies. The senior Scouts know that the new boy is instructed to wake the Patrol leader if he gets cold. The patrol leader is then to get up and help build the fire. No wood, no matches, etc., are not excuses to be used to awaken the sleeping Scoutmaster.

However, the senior Scouts soon learn that new adult leaders will invariably have sympathy for a cold 11 year old, and will get up, build him a fire, heat some hot chocolate, and perhaps have enough left over for others who are awake. For years the patrol leaders have made sure that a new dad goes along on the Polar Bear campouts. The list of dads who have been suckered with this trick by the patrol leaders is endless.

One crisp January morning I crawled out of my pine bough lean-to after eight hours of warm and comfortable sleep to find my Assistant Scoutmaster, Gary Hollensteiner, sitting bleary eyed by a fire with a couple of young Scouts. That was the third fire that night that he had been conned into starting. For years, every time one of our Scouts would see Gary on the street he would greet him with, "Mr. Holly (they shortened Hollensteiner) build me a fire. I'm cold."

Particularly enjoyable is working with new Scouts on their first progress award. They are usually eager and anxious to learn, wanting to complete the requirements for Eagle Scout in a couple of weeks at the outside.

On one camp-out I took four new Scouts aside to work on the portion of the Tenderfoot requirement which dealt with the Outdoor Code. We had a sack lunch to take along to eat while working on the requirement. A beautiful site was chosen, overlooking the Little Muskegon River in Newaygo County, Michigan, which was well away from the campsite and the older Scouts.

The session went well, and I was proud of myself for having effectively gotten the conservationist's message across to these boys. My feeling was reinforced as we were walking back to camp, and one boy emphatically stated, "We really gotta do something about this pollution stuff, or the whole world will be one big garbage dump." Seconds later my ego was shattered as the same kid heaved his empty soda can into the bushes. You can rest assured that, after I blew my cool, he was careful not to litter (or at least not to get caught) for the remainder of the camp-out.

Kids are all different. I guess that is what makes them so much fun to work with. No two are alike. Each is an individual with his own personality. What turns one on, turns another off. A secret to success as a youth leader is to treat each boy as an individual. Trying to make all boys fit the same mold just doesn't work.

But there are many things that all boys seem to have in common. For one thing, it is almost impossible to con a kid. Adults can be strung along till the cows come home, but for some unknown reason a kid can always tell when a person is really sincere, and when he is being phony. I have found that it is always best to be completely honest and truthful with a boy, even if the truth sometimes hurts. The leader who functions out of a sense of responsbility rather than a desire to help boys is rarely effective.

There are some kids who go sour in spite of a positive environment. Others are successes in spite of a very inferior environment. But as a general rule, I believe that most kids are a product of the environment in which they are reared. I believe that a good example can do more than anything else to promote the spirit of the golden rule among Scouts. Boys of Scouting age continually watch the activities of their troop leaders, not only at troop meetings, but everyday in community life. Scouts will, to some extent, adopt the attitudes of the adults with whom they are associated, the Scoutmaster being one of these adults. All of the preaching, teaching, and encouraging that a Scoutmaster can do to promote favorable behavior will not do half the good that a positive example will do. It seems almost universal that a boy wants to please those people whom he respects. This can be a valuable tool for any adult to use (or abuse).

A mother tells her son not to use drugs but meets her husband at the door each evening with a martini. A father can't understand why his son was caught shoplifting, even though he himself brings paper and pencils home from the office for the kids to use at school. The boy is forced to eat his vegetables because they are good for him, as the parent continues to smoke a pack, of cigarettes a day. Come on parents—wake up! You can fool your spouse, and you can even pretend to fool yourself, but you can't fool your kid.

Photo Courtesy of Jim Boeger

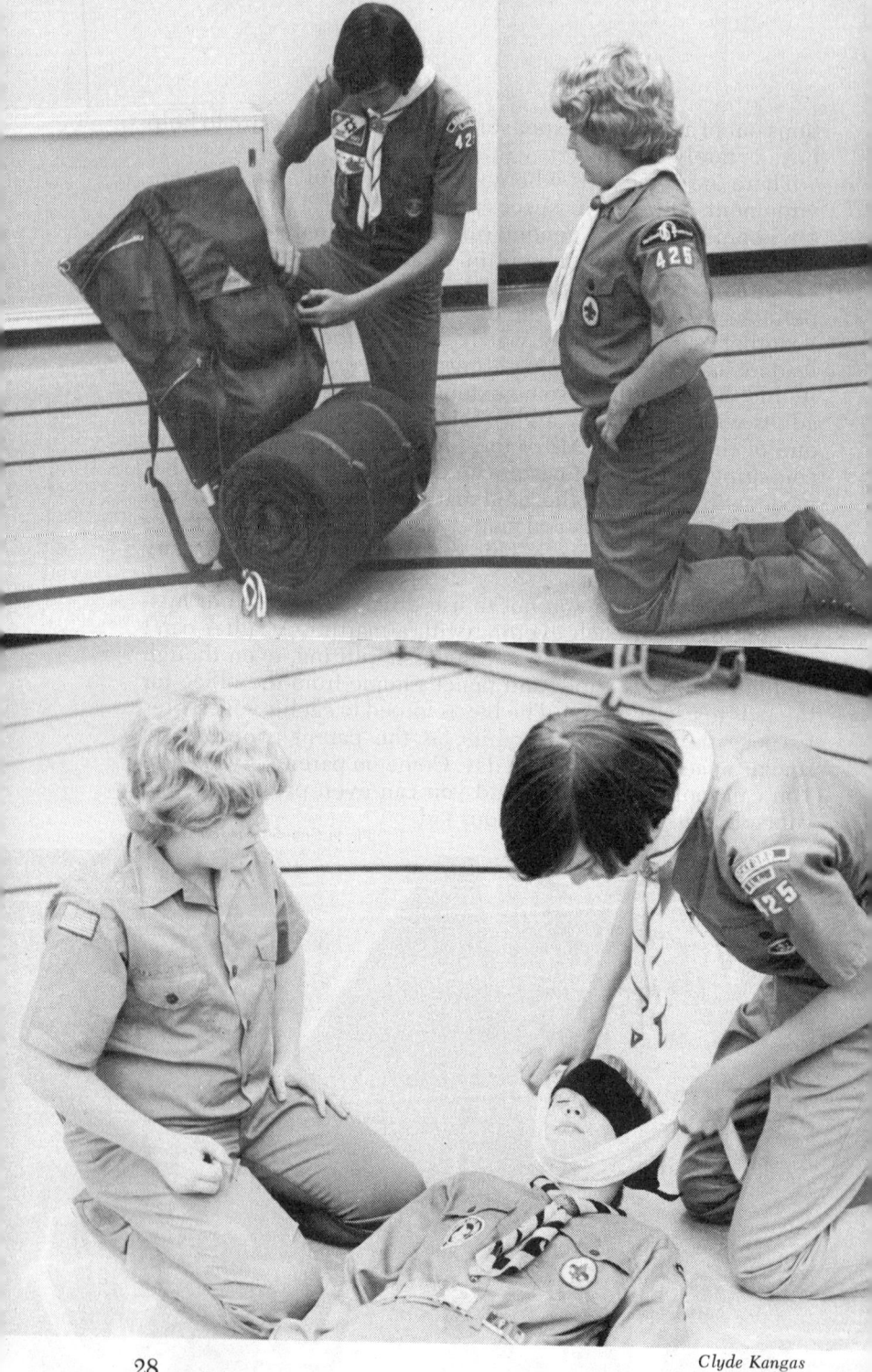

Clyde Kangas

Chapter 3

The Scouting Program

There is nothing magic about the Scouting program. It is just a group of hard working, dedicated men (and women) trying to teach boys how to become successful and responsible adults. One should not expect any miracles out of the Scouting program. There is no guarantee that the troublesome boy will enter Scouting at 11 years of age and emerge a few years later as a Presidential candidate. The program offered by each individual troop greatly reflects the leadership of the Scoutmaster. Thus the quality of the program varies everywhere from excellent to terrible. One should not assume that just because your church or school has a Scout troop, it has a strong and effective Scouting program. There is no substitute for the parental responsibility to investigate the qualifications of the Scoutmaster and the type of program being offered to the boys of a particular troop.

The Scouting program in America is coordinated by a group of paid professional Scouters. The United States is divided into regions, councils, and districts. A paid professional district executive is responsible for coordinating the Scouting program in each district.

Local council volunteers, supported by regional and national Scouting professionals and volunteers, provide the back up resources that individual troops and packs cannot provide for themselves. They also provide the facilities which are beyond the means of individual troops and packs, such as camps. It is the many friends of Scouting who provide the financial support needed for the administration personnel, the facilities, and the record keeping function. These administrative people see that the tools are made available to support the program of the individual Scout troops and Cub packs.

And then the people actually responsible for taking the program to the boys are the unit leaders, primarily the Scoutmasters and Cubmasters, backed by Den Mothers, Committee Chairmen, Scouting Coordinators, etc.,—all volunteers held together by a common goal.

The troop program usually consists of weekly troop meetings, patrol meetings (several patrols per troop), a monthly outdoor activity, and a week long summer camping experience.

As stated elsewhere in this text, the three aims of the program are character development, citizenship training, and the development of physical and mental fitness. The outdoor emphasis is just one of the tools used to achieve these three aims.

The advancement program is another tool. A Scout can progress in Scouting from the beginning progress award of Scout, up through Tenderfoot, Second Class, First Class, Star, Life, and finally Eagle, the highest award. The requirements for each progress award become increasingly difficult when compared with the one before. Scouts can work on their progress awards at their own pace, thus allowing them to set their own goals and follow through on their own initiative. About 1% of the Scouts achieve the rank of Eagle Scout. Does this mean that the other 99% are failures? No, certainly not, for every phase of the Scouting program is a learning experience. The advancement program does force a Scout (if he wants to advance) to perform community service projects, to demonstrate his leadership ability, and to take initiative on his own. The merit badge program, an important part of the advancement program, gives the Scout the opportunity to meet many interesting and knowledgeable people he otherwise would not have been able to meet. He is exposed to community experts in fields such as fingerprinting, space exploration, computers, first aid, and many others. There are over 120 merit badges that a Scout can choose to earn. It is a little frightening for an eleven year old the first time he must call a merit badge counselor, a complete stranger, and ask for an appointment. The second and third times usually get a little easier. Advancement is only one part of Scouting. Failure to advance certainly does not mean failure as a Scout. Unfortunately a few leaders confuse the Scouting program with the advancement program.

The use of the patrol method is another important tool of the Scouting program. Boys are divided into small groups (patrols) of 6-10 in each. They are allowed to function as a small democracy, each having a representative voice in troop decisions. Each patrol is led by a patrol leader where leadership responsibilities are learned, sometimes the hard way through the school of hard knocks.

Once in a while a misguided leader will train a group of boy leaders to the point where they are really working together great; where they have learned how to lead, and are doing an effective job of it. So far so good. All good leaders try to pull this off. But then the misguided ones try to maintain this leadership structure several years so that their job is made easier. The point is to train boys to be leaders, not to maintain good leaders in their present leadership capacities indefinitely. Train new boys. Let the older boys train the new boys. Let the new leaders make some mistakes. Boys will never learn to be leaders by watching films or listening to lectures but will by actually doing the job. Whenever a Scoutmaster thinks that his boy leaders are really doing a great job, it is time to bring in younger boys, and start the learning process all over again. Hopefully this process will be a continual one with effective boy leaders teaching the younger Scouts.

Few people are born with leadership capability, but many can be trained to carry leadership responsibility. The job is not easy and doesn't happen without hard effort. It would almost always be easier for the Scoutmaster to do a job himself than to sit back and watch a new patrol leader fumble around trying to be a leader and a buddy at the same time, not really understanding the difference between the two. If given a chance, the saying, "Teach them, trust them, and let them lead," will yield good results. Our younger generation can indeed accept leadership responsibilities at a relatively young age if we will just have confidence in them.

Above all, the Scouting program must be fun. A boy only becomes a Scout because he wants to, not because he is required by law. Learning experiences, service projects, leadership responsibilities, etc., can all be a lot of fun if presented in the right light.

Responsibility is another trait that does not just happen, but that must be learned, usually by example from others. I have watched boys head for cars after a camp-out leaving a fire going, and junk scattered over the campsite. Negligent? No, they knew better, but they also knew that I was there and that it was my responsibility to see that things were done, not theirs. Two weeks later I saw these same boys leave a spotless campsite when I intentionally disappeared for an hour or so during camp breaking. There was no one else to shoulder the responsibility for them, thus they accepted it and did an admirable job of fulfilling their responsibilities.

It is a pleasant experience watching a sense of responsibility develop within a boy. Sometimes one can see him mature almost overnight. Kevin Phillips proved himself to be worthy of the challenge during a Polar Bear Camporee a couple years ago. Jim Douglas, their Scoutmaster, became ill and had to leave soon after camp was pitched. I agreed to be responsible for Jim's troop in his absence. They were on the next campsite, so I knew that I couldn't provide constant supervision and leadership to both his and my troops. Kevin was the oldest Scout present, so I gave him full responsibility for handling his troop the rest of the weekend. From a distance it was a pleasure to watch him change from one of the group to the leader of the group. His leadership was effective (not bossy), and the other boys followed his lead without question. His willingness to work with them, and harder than any one of them, was the clincher that won him their confidence. Not all boys can or want to accept the responsibilities of leadership, but those who do are given the opportunity in the Scouting program.

Over the years I have met quite a variety of men wearing the badge of the Scoutmaster. They are not held together by race, religion, ethnic background, income, age, or education, but by an interest in helping and being around boys. Within a few minutes at one of the high adventure bases, I met a Scoutmaster who was president of a major industrial corporation and another who couldn't read. The background is not nearly as important as the influence he has on the boys in his troop.

While there is a *Scout Handbook,* and a *Scoutmaster's Handbook,* telling how to organize, coordinate, train, etc., an ideal troop in accordance with the accepted program of the Boy Scouts of America, from a practical standpoint, every Scoutmaster tailors his program to where he is comfortable with it. The aims are the same, but the techniques used are different to suit the personalities of the characters involved.

For example, Scoutmaster Ralph Thieman tries to see that his troop runs by the book and is very successful, having an excellent Scouting program. Scoutmaster Ed Gengenbacher has been criticised for running a boys club, not a Scouting program, just because he always does all the cooking. True, the book says that under the patrol method, the boys should do their own cooking by patrols. But remember, this is only a small part of the Scouting program. The patrol method provides individual boys the opportunity to gain practical leadership experience in many places other than in the "camp kitchen." The boys of Troop 22 love their "Mr. Ed" for the fine example he has set for them through the years, and he in turn does his best to help each one of them on an individual basis. The boys of St. Francis Parish are going to be better men for having known a Scoutmaster like Ed Gengenbacher. So what if they still can't cook?

The Scouting program as it is today has evolved over the years. The leaders of this organization realize that change is absolutely necessary if any movement is going to continue to prosper. National Scouting program planners have made every attempt to keep the Scouting program current with the needs of today's youth. When drugs started to become a major problem in the late 1960's, they tried to combat it with Operation Reach, which was an attempt to open boy-parent communication channels. It was a "preventive maintenance" program aimed at eliminating the need for boys to experiment with drugs. As urban populations have increased, the program has been expanded to provide for the boy trapped in the asphalt jungle. As with change in any organization, it is possible for some of the "improvements" to turn sour. Fortunately our

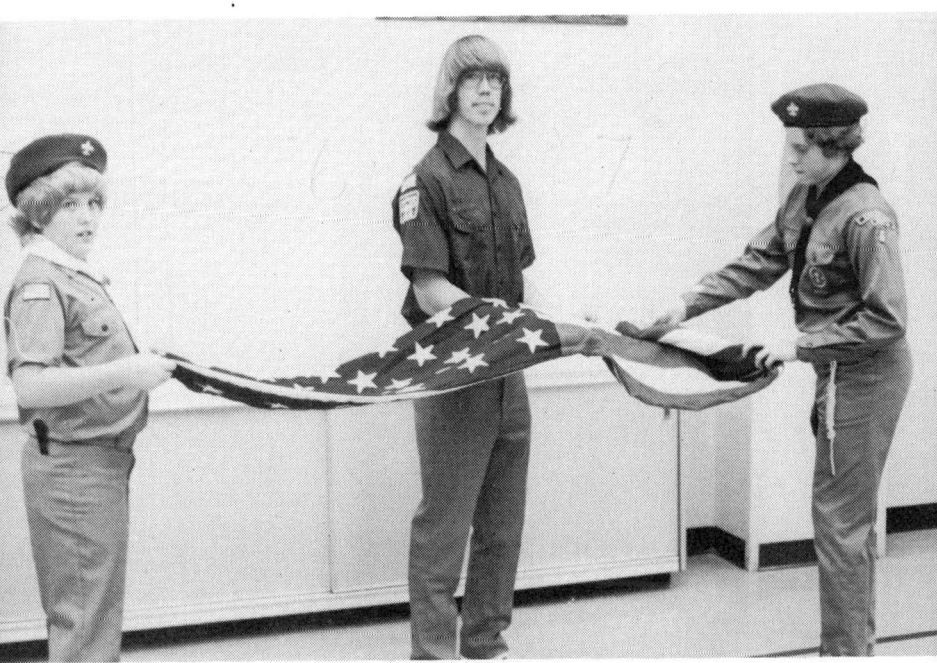

Clyde Kangas

Scouting leaders are also not afraid to recognize and admit to mistakes and attempt to correct them.

One cannot expect to be able to build a bridge until after he has mastered the principles of civil engineering. Likewise one cannot expect to be able to wire a house until he has learned the principles of electricity through proper training. To be an effective Scout leader also requires proper training. True, a new leader can stumble along without the advantage of training courses, but the job certainly becomes easier and more enjoyable after attending the series of adult leader training sessions. Wood Badge, a training program for adult Scouters, has been expanded to the point where it is now readily available to every man who wants to take the time to learn from experienced leaders what this Scouting game is all about.

I will not bore you with any facts and figures about the Scouting program. I am sure you can read other books or articles which go into the specifics of the Scouting program in any amount of detail. I would encourage you to become familiar with it. In my personal opinion, I believe that only the communist and the atheist can find serious fault with the aims and objectives of the Scouting program.

Clyde Kangas

Chapter 4
Scouting Builds Character

Kids can be monsters at times. There are those days when they are boisterous, obnoxious, selfish, belligerent, stubborn, cantankerous—you name it and kids have been it at one time or another. One attempt to hold a troop meeting the night after the last day of school in June proved to be a pure disaster. Knot tying was the last thing on their minds. I don't believe they even realized that, out of sheer desperation, the troop meeting was ended thirty minutes ahead of the regular closing time. About half of the kids seem to go through the know-it-all fourteen, lazy fifteen, and sassy sixteen stages. But then just about when you are ready to give up on them they seem to come through with some out of character deed that makes you think that there just might be some hope for them yet.

Perhaps one of the reasons I like to work with Scout age boys is that they are willing to accept new ideas. Their values and beliefs are not yet set in the concrete. It seems like the older we get the more set in our ways we become. But the Scout age boy can still be positively influenced with a good example (or a bad one), can still mold his behavior, and can still change his values, which he will be carrying with him for the rest of his life. I like to be a part of this molding process.

A lot of money has been donated to the Scouting program across the country in the past several decades by parents, by industry, by "rich sugar daddies" and average citizens alike, and for what? Does it really do any good? Why give another buck, next year?

Yes, I personally believe that the program of the Boy Scouts of America does provide the opportunity to develop the character of our young men. No, we are not successful with every Scout and never will be, but there are a few who have had their lives changed because of the positive influence of a dedicated Scout leader. If the world was filled with perfect, loving parents, we probably would not need Scouting for anything but a babysitting function. But unfortunately such is not the case. Far too often the family life of our Scouts is not a mirror image of The Waltons. Too many parents just don't care. Too many don't want to take the time. Too many don't remember their needs when they were eleven years old.

The Scoutmaster is indeed in a unique position to influence the character of a boy. From the vantage point of a teenager, parents, of course, don't know anything. They are twenty years behind the times, and sometimes just not very bright. Teachers and ministers are being paid to do their thing. Again, from the vantage point of the teenager, they may be more interested in earning the paycheck than in really helping. But the Scout leader, soccer coach, youth fellowship counselor, plus many other youth volunteers, are donating their time, so must be sincere in their relationship with boys. The magnetic attraction and influence between a boy seeking someone to look up to, and a youth leader interested in youth, can be strong and lasting.

It was a cold and snowy Monday night in Grand Haven, Michigan, and an officer from the local Coast Guard station had been invited to demonstrate mouth to mouth resuscitation at our troop meeting. I thought the snow would keep a few of the marginally interested boys home, but was confident of a good turnout at the meeting.

At the regular starting time only a handful of Scouts had drifted into the meeting room. I pretended not to be concerned, and continued to kill time talking with the Coast Guard officer. Twenty minutes later there was still only a handful of Scouts and none of the senior Scouts present. Needless to say it was very embarrassing to have invited a guest to the troop meeting to present a program and have no one show up. I really couldn't understand where the rest of the crew could be.

At 7:35 p.m., in came the rest of the troop altogether, laughing, throwing snowballs, and generally raising cain. I was biting nails by that time. I didn't know where they had been, but was sure that they had been up to no good.

Soon the story came out that they had decided at school earlier in the afternoon to meet at the home of the former Scoutmaster to shovel the snow from his sidewalk. He had suffered a heart attack two weeks earlier. Suddenly I couldn't have been more proud of "my" boys. The Coast Guard officer joked that had he known a good turn like that was happening, he would have brought his shovel.

Does an event like that just happen by itself? No, it takes years of good example by parents, teachers, ministers, friends, peers, relatives, youth leaders, and even complete strangers to develop the character within each individual that makes him want to help others, and feel good about having done a good turn.

Whenever our troop is camping on a Sunday morning, we provide a Protestant worship service for the Scouts. Initially we tried getting everyone in uniform and heading to a local church near our camp. It soon became obvious that most of the boys weren't really getting much out of the services. It was too much like going to church back home where Mom and Dad forced you to sit still and be quiet.

One weekend after a cold Polar Bear camp, we stopped to attend church in Lewistown, Missouri. The temperature was in the mid-twenties all weekend, and it had been 24 hours since any of us were inside a heated building. The congregation, mostly senior citizens, was quite small. It must have been eighty degrees in that building. That hot building and a long-winded preacher were all our crew needed to put them fast asleep. Halfway through the sermon I gave up poking and punching, trying to keep them awake.

After that, we decided to hold our own worship services while camping. This has proved to be very effective, and hopefully beneficial. Sometimes the worship will be led by the Scoutmaster or one of the other adult leaders, and sometimes the boys are put in charge of the service.

After camping for the weekend at Wakonda State Park near LaGrange, Missouri, we got the troop together for our Sunday morning worship service on a small sandy knoll near the campsite. It had been another cold January campout. The wind was pretty stiff, and a freezing rain was starting to fall. We wanted to get home before the highways started to get slick. It was very tempting to say, "the heck with it," bundle into the cars, and take off for the barn. The last thing most wanted to do was sit in the sand in a cold freezing rain and listen to a sermon. I really didn't blame them.

But I decided to have a short service, getting to the amen

line faster than originally planned. My topic for the morning was on the use of alcohol, a sermon which I have used a couple of times since. As I was talking, I thought of what a waste of time this was. Everyone was too busy thinking of how cold and wet he was, not of anything that I was saying. I might as well have been howling at the moon. I hardly got the *a* of *amen* out when the mad dash to the cars was on. I must admit that I was right behind the pack.

The reward for that day came five years later. A college freshman stopped by the house to visit one afternoon. In the conversation he indicated that alcohol was not going to be a problem for him at college due to that sermon five years earlier on a cold, wet sandy knoll at Wakonda State Park. One never knows how far, or for how long his individual sphere of influence will extend.

It was a good week at summer camp. We had arrived at Saukenauk Scout Reservation on a Sunday afternoon and would be heading back to Quincy the following Saturday. By Wednesday the boys were making good progress on their merit badges, nobody was homesick, it hadn't rained too much, and we had managed to catch a raccoon in a garbage can. Tom had some poison ivy, Dave was covered with chigger bites, and someone had cleaned a fish right behind Dennis' tent, but other than that things were progressing nicely.

Things were routine at Thursday's breakfast in Gardner Lodge until Camp Director Arnold Ludwig got up to speak. It seems that the night before someone had put eggs in the sleeping bag of a new Scout in Troop 56, camped on the ridge adjacent to our site. The guilty culprit had not been found. Fun is OK, but damage to property is something else.

That morning, using the Scout Law as the guide, Arnold Ludwig gave a very effective talk about the responsibilities of a Scout. He was not on a witch hunt, did not threaten to punish the guilty party, but appealed to the pride of every boy present that this conduct was not acceptable. You could have heard a pin drop in the dining hall.

After nosing around and talking with a few of our senior Scouts, I was pretty sure that none of our Troop had been involved in the egg incident. The guilty party was not found that summer.

Recently, a fellow Scoutmaster related to me that three years later, a boy, after receiving his Eagle Scout Award and graduating from high school, had come over to his home, and admitted to having put the eggs in the sleeping bag. For three years that incident had been gnawing on his conscience, and

I guess he finally had to be honest with himself. The fruits of labor are sometimes long in coming, but character is indeed developed in the Scouting program.

The program available at the High Adventure Bases is excellent, in my opinion. To the Scout, the Philmont program is fun, hard work, hiking, camping, cooking, campfires, and taking part in staff conducted programs. As an adult, it is obvious that there is a specific learning experience connected with almost every aspect of the Philmont program.

There was what is referred to as an interpretive program at Clear Creek Camp. The staff at that particular camp looked like, lived like, and sometimes even smelled like mountain men from the high country. The Rocky Mountain Fur Trading Company they called themselves. The program they presented to the boys was to depict life like it was a century ago in the high country where fur trapping and trading was the way of life. I don't believe that our crew ever was really sure if those men were Philmont staff, or mountain men whom we had stumbled onto by accident. They did an excellent job of showing the boys how animals were trapped, and how to shoot the old black powder rifles.

One of the mountain men called himself Hawkeye. He wore a big floppy hat, buckskin pants with suspenders, and no shirt. He always had a big knife suspended from his belt right in the middle of his back. Hawkeye was indeed a rough looking individual. He spoke and acted like he had been hardened by years of trying to scratch out a living doing battle with Mother Nature up there in the backwoods and high country of the Rocky Mountains. At first the boys were a little shy about going up and talking with that rough looking individual.

That afternoon I was comfortably propped against a tree on the slope above Clear Creek Camp, just taking in some rays, and resting my trail tired feet. Below I saw Hawkeye come out of the cabin, sit on the edge of the porch, and start whittling on a stick. Pretty soon a lone Scout came up, sat down, and joined in the whittling. Before long a couple dozen Scouts were gathered around the porch of that old cabin listening to that mountain man tell tales of days gone by.

Hawkeye joked with the boys that they probably thought he looked different and weird the first time they saw him. Of course the boys denied it saying, "No, we didn't think you were weird." With that denial, Hawkeye grabbed the boy closest to him by the shirt, and in the meanest voice he could muster shouted, "You did too. You thought I was some kind of a freak the first time you laid eyes on me now didn't you?" Practically in fear for his life, the boy, of course, agreed that he had thought Hawkeye a little different. In a low voice which caused every Scout to strain to hear every word, Hawkeye continued saying that we often distrust things or people whom we don't really know. But if we really get to know a person, regardless of his race, religion, nationality, etc., we will almost always like him. The moral of the story, of course, being that our world would be a better place in which to live if we would get to know people personally before we criticize them. The story was soon dropped in favor of other tales of tangles with "griz," skunks, Injuns, etc.

A week later we were on our way home after a great expedition at Philmont. We were spending the night in Newton, Kansas. There were a few hours of daylight left, so we found the public swimming pool in an attempt to combat the Kansas summer heat.

After swimming we were all loading back into the cars when a young black man was spotted crossing the street about half a block away. He was wearing violet tight pants, a bright green silk shirt, pointed shoes, and a pink five gallon hat adorned with a big blue feather. For our conservative small town midwestern boys, he was a sight to behold. One of our Scouts started to snicker, "Look at that spook all duded up." Then from the back seat Mark spoke, "Remember what Hawkeye said? He might be a good guy if we got to know him." There was a moment of silence, and the incident passed without comment.

Even bad experiences and harsh discipline can be beneficial and growing experiences for boys. The worst camp-out that I was ever on was a recent spring camporee. For some reason I was the only adult with the troop on this particular weekend. While this was not a desirable situation, such was the case.

I don't know if it was the weather, the phase of the moon, or just plain orneriness, but the boys didn't seem to be doing anything right this weekend. The big ones were picking on the little ones, there were squabbles over who was going to do the dishes, some didn't want to take part in the program, etc. Frankly I had just about had it when night finally came.

It was a short night! About 3:00 A.M. I heard a commotion in the campsite. That was the last straw. Investigation showed a tent collapsed on a couple of the younger Scouts. Fooling with tents or personal property is absolutely forbidden, and all of the Scouts knew the rules well. With fire in my eyes, the troop was ordered to fall into formation. After an uncomplimentary speech, I asked the guilty Scouts to step forward. Five boys, slowly stepped forward and admitted to causing the ruckus. In spite of being angry, I was proud that they were men enough to stand up and admit their guilt, and I told them so. But the question remained of what to do now that they had admitted their crime at 3:00 A.M. in the morning. To send them back to bed would have set a bad example for the other Scouts, and to send them home would have been a little harsh. By this time I was wide awake and cooled down a little.

It was a nice night, so why not take a hike. Our five rambunctious turks were politely requested to don their hiking boots, requisition a flashlight, and meet at my tent in five minutes. It was obvious that they were tired, so they must have been awake most of the night planning their caper. At 3:15 A.M. I headed off over the hills of Saukenauk at a good healthy pace. My pace caused some of them almost to run to keep up. A couple of times I almost started to feel sorry for them but kept going nevertheless. Just as light started to appear in the eastern sky, I brought them dragging back into camp. As they started to head for their tents, the bad news was issued that it was now time to start building the fires for breakfast. We kept those boys on their feet all the rest of the day. It almost killed me to stay awake, but I didn't dare let them know that. Needless to say we all got a good eight hours of sleep the next night.

Scouts don't mind discipline when they know that it is deserved. In fact I believe that they expect it and are disappointed if discipline is too loose. All five of those boys still will mention on occasion the "time we hiked all night."

One winter the youth of our church conducted the Sunday morning worship service for the congregation. Most of the boys that participated in the worship service were also Scouts in Troop 9. That particular morning the theme of their service was "being available to help others in time of need," which was centered around the parable of The Good Samaritan. The service went well, and I left with a good feeling about our youth and their willingness to stand up and tell the whole world about their belief in God.

At about eight o'clock that night I received a call for help. There was a ten-year-old boy lost near Canton, Missouri, and a search effort was being organized. I didn't want to try to coordinate our whole troop on a cold, dark night, but knew some of the older Scouts could handle the search effort. I called a handful of the older boys, and within minutes my van was loaded and headed for Canton, some twenty miles away. Just as I went out of the door I looked at the thermometer, and it stood right at zero.

The search effort was being organized at Ben's Cycle Shop on the south edge of town. The home where I grew up was on the hill just above the cycle shop. I knew every inch of this country in a five mile radius. I could remember when I was ten years old I knew every ant hill, ground hog hole, and squirrel nest around, and could have found my way home blindfolded. But this boy had only lived here for a few months. Looking back twenty years I tried to remember those places that were my favorites: where darkness often crept up before I knew it. My two favorite places to spend a winter afternoon had been along the banks of the Wyaconda River, a mile and a half to the west, and along the Mississippi River bank, half a mile to the east. Naturally I had been forbidden to play along the Mississippi, which made it even more appealing. The Mississippi River bank would have the thickest underbrush and would be the hardest place to search, so I volunteered our crew to handle that section.

At first it was exciting to our boys. They thought taking part in a search effort was great. We could see flashlights speckle the bluffs above us to the west where other search parties were working. The going was really rough. The underbrush, vines, and debris were even thicker than I had remembered. We were spaced close together so as to be able to cover every inch of ground. The Scout on the east end of the line was the coldest, for the wind coming off the Mississippi was really sharp. By now the temperature must have dropped below zero. I couldn't help but think how frightening it must be to that lost boy to be out in a night as cold and dark as this one.

About midnight a couple of our boys started to complain about being cold and tired. We took a break, and gathered around in a circle. I simply asked them, "Did you really mean what you were saying this morning in church about being available to help others in time of need?" There was silence, and then the complainer jumped to his feet and said, "Let's hit it gang." I believe that they would have stayed out in that brush looking all night had I let them. We covered every inch of ground along four miles of River shore before deciding to return to the search headquarters. It was nearing 3:00 A.M., and I decided it was time I got our boys home.

The boy was found early the next morning by the Wyaconda River. He was cold and scared, but unhurt. While our Scouts didn't find the boy, I believe that they all had a good feeling about having tried to help and having done their best.

Boys seem to grow the most when the challenge is the hardest. Being able to accomplish the extraordinary sets one a little apart from everybody else. Hardships on camp-outs present those challenges which cause boys to extend themselves beyond those limits in which they feel comfortable.

The Blackhawk District 1972 Polar Bear Camporee was just such an event. The weekend started out clear and crisp with the temperature near zero. That was enough to hold the attendance down a little I thought, but was surprised when only three troops out of a probable thirty showed up. I believe that every worried mother in the troop had called me earlier in the morning with the question, "You aren't really going camping today, are you?" The kids didn't seem to be the least bit concerned about the cold weather. The lake had frozen smooth this year so ice skating was great. The first order of business was to put up a dining fly as a wind shield and build a big fire. The wood supply was soon collected, and it was almost warm while sitting between the fire and the canvas wind shield.

The temperature continued to slowly drop all day until it reached five degrees below at supper time. Cooking wasn't much of a problem, but getting dishes done proved to be difficult. Wet hands and five degrees below zero are not a good combination. The boys stayed warm all day while active, but now that it was getting dark, it seemed even colder than ever.

Clyde Kangas

The forecast called for the temperature to continue to drop all night.

The decision was made to move all of the boys into the dining hall until the next morning. It was not heated, but there was a huge stone fireplace in one end of the building. The concrete floor was just too cold to have kids sleep on, so we moved all of the tables together in the middle of the room, making one big platform. Soon all fifty kids were bedded down in one big pile of humanity on the tables. It never did get above freezing in the dining hall, but was better than the twelve below to which it dropped out-of-doors.

We have had great weather for other Polar Bear Camporees, but none made as much of an impression on our boys' memories as the night we all slept on the tables in Gardner Lodge.

Every one of us is surrounded by what I will call an invisible sphere of influence. Our actions and deeds every day influence the lives of other people. One would be surprised if he really knew just how many different people are aware of his actions every day. A boy does not learn about smoking pot or shoplifting except through the example of others. A boy does not learn about doing volunteer work at the nursing home or about how to pray except through the example of others. How has your example been today?

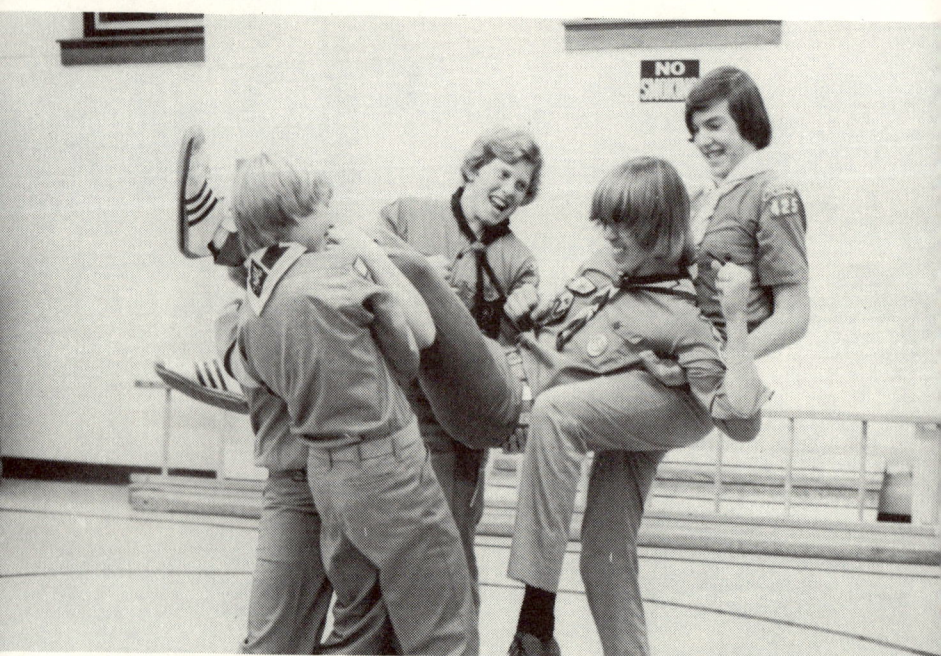

Clyde Kangas

Chapter 5

Why Bother?

The first time I was faced with a sub-freezing camp-out, it was a real challenge. Could we make it? Could we keep warm enough? How would we get the tent pegs to stay in? Would we have to take turns all night keeping the fire going? After ten years of cold weather camping, most of the challenge of nature is gone. It is easy to be lulled into the complacency of thinking of the coming weekend as just another cold camp-out. So why bother? I'll tell you why.

The youth of today need guidance more than ever before. Today's newspapers are filled with stories of youth in trouble. These stories originate from Park Avenue to Ghetto Lane; from New York City to Podunk Junction; from large and small families alike; and deal with all races and religions.

Television lays the troubles of the world right out in front of today's teenagers like never before. Parents are busy holding down two jobs to keep up with the Jones's or with inflation. Moral standards are probably at an all-time low, drugs and dope are easily available for experimentation to such an extent that alcohol is brushed off as, "no big problem" any more, pollution will wipe us out; the Communists will bomb us out; the "establishment" will dictate over us; and on and on. The list is endless. Teenagers today are faced with all of the above problems that were only mentioned by the teenagers of two generations ago.

The teenagers of today will be the men guiding our country

and our destiny tomorrow. The attitudes that they develop now will be reflected in the way they lead their adult lives. I strongly believe that teenagers today, as in all ages past, are basically good. However, they need guidance more than ever in differentiating right from wrong; good from bad. Given strong guidance and a good example, I believe these teenagers have the intelligence to make their own decisions, and make them right.

To me, Scouting is the one small way that I hope to exert my influence on the character of a few boys. Scouting is not teaching knots or having fun at a campfire but is an attempt, at least for me, to develop tomorrow's adult citizens and leaders.

As long as I believe that I am doing some good and possibly contributing to the character development of even one boy, I want to continue in Scouting. There are many avenues today through which this could be accomplished, including the church organizations, school functions, Big Brother programs, and many others. I choose to continue to work in Scouting primarily because I enjoy it. I enjoy working with and being around young boys of Scout age, and I strongly believe in the basic aims of Scouting which include citizenship training, character development, and the maintaining of strong physical and mental health.

Several summers ago Chris Cook and I took a group of Scouts for a week-long canoe trip to Region Seven Canoe Base near Boulder Junction, Wisconsin. Five of the boys were from our troop. You wouldn't really call them "rich kids," but none of them ever had to worry about where the next meal was coming from. The other five were from Troop 90, sponsored by Indian Hills Housing Development. All were good kids, but there was an obvious difference between the personalities and personal values of the two groups of boys.

On the way home after a rainy but enjoyable canoe trip, we pulled into a roadside park to hold a short worship service. Our Scouts knew this was traditional on Sunday morning. While they may not have been overly excited at the prospect, they knew that any arguments would fall on disapproving ears, so accepted the stop as a fact of life. A couple of the Troop 90 Scouts grumbled about having gone fifteen years without church, so why have to start now? With a little coaxing, all soon joined us at a couple of picnic tables near the far edge of the park.

The discussion this particular Sunday morning was about the golden rule. Steve was sitting with his head in his folded arms, leaning over the table, pretending to be bored with the proceedings. After the golden rule was mentioned several times Steve cocked his head to one side and asked, "What's that?" I had assumed that all the boys would know what the golden rule was but obviously was mistaken. "Do unto others as you would have others do unto you" was then explained. After a moment of silence, Steve shook his head saying, "It ain't never goin' to work."

The Vietnam war was at its peak. Steve illustrated what he meant with, "If a Viet Cong soldier is shooting at you, being nice to him isn't going to get you anything but killed."

Perhaps Steve was right, but personally I prefer to believe in the golden rule, and want to continue to do everything I can to assure that the next generation can also believe in the merit of following it in everyday life. Why can't the whole world believe in it? Have you done anything today to reinforce Steve's belief that, "It ain't never goin' to work"? Have you done anything today to demonstrate to the next generation that it does indeed work?

Scouting seems to attract "good men." Most of the Scouters whom I have met across the country have been hard working, friendly, and cooperative persons with values and a purpose in life similar to my own. I wish that I could tell of hundreds of such men with whom I am acquainted, but time and space just will not allow it.

Former Scoutmaster Basil Williams is probably the epitome of the image that represents the dedicated Scouter. Just last year I watched as Basil was presented his fifty-year service star which represents fifty years of dedicated service to the youth of our country. Basil is now well up into his 70s and still serves as Nature Director at Saukenauk Scout Reservation every summer.

Last July, I was helping other Scoutmasters complain about the heat while enjoying a glass of iced tea in Gardner Lodge. It was one of those miserably hot and humid days without a breath of air stirring that are so typical of the Mississippi River valley in July. In bounced Basil, chuckling to himself. In spite of the heat he had a spring to his gait and was wearing a watermelon smile, "I fooled them today," was his comment. One of my fellow Scoutmasters couldn't resist asking, "Who did you fool today Basil?" His reply could have been predicted. "The doctors of course. They told me to hold my activity down to one five mile hike a day, but I fooled them today. I took two five-mile hikes."

Basil is like the Pied Piper. He can start out talking to himself fondling a leaf. Soon one lone Scout will stop to see what he is doing. Within five minutes, Basil is off through the woods explaining every tree and bush in sight, with half the Scouts on the reservation hot on his heels, straining to hear every golden word. He has the unusual knack for teaching boys that few people have the good fortune of acquiring.

It was a hot Webelos weekend in June when I introduced John Green to Basil. John has since become one of the most active black Scouters in the Saukee Area Council. John is a big man. He stands well over 6 feet, and must weigh 250 if he weighs an ounce. It is solid muscle and bone. While he has a heart made of gold, because of his size and build, you just automatically say, "Yes Sir" when you first meet John.

On this particular weekend, John was new to Scouting. Basil was just about to take the Webelos on a nature hike. John's ten year old son was trying to talk his Dad into going along. I encouraged, "This guy is good on nature hikes. I think that you would enjoy it, John." John still thought it was a pretty hot day to be traipsing over the hills just to hear about trees and stuff. I teased, "Come on John, surely you can keep up with that 70 year old man." John finally collapsed under his son's pressure and took off down the trail after Basil and crew.

Two hours and five miles later, Basil came ambling up over the hill looking fresh as a daisy, with his crew still in tow. Last in line and starting to fall behind was John Green, soaked with sweat, mopping his sweaty brow with a soaked handkerchief. John came over to me with the question, "Who is that man?" I thought that I was about to be chewed out for conning John into going along on the hike, but instead John spent the next fifteen minutes telling me what a great job Basil did working with the kids introducing them to some of the wonders of nature.

Another inspiration to his fellow Scouters is Sy Runkel from Des Moines, whom I met on the trails at Philmont. When I first saw Sy coming up the trail toward us, I thought it must be a mirage. There was no way this man could make it eleven days and fifty miles through those mountains with full pack. He was obviously no spring chicken, leaned on a walking stick for support, and was favoring a stiff leg.

Several campfires and many miles later I came to admire this man for what he was—another man dedicated to serving the youth of our country. The stiff leg he received from a German bullet while serving as a glider pilot in World War II. He was retired from public service as a conservationist. This was his second high adventure expedition for the summer, having taken his Explorer Post backpacking over Isle Royale National Park the previous month. At the end of the trail, I believe Sy was in better shape than I.

If every boy had a man like Basil or Sy to look up to as an example, I wonder what our world would be like?

I have never seen a good cause that died for lack of funds. If a cause, regardless of what it is, is genuinely good and worthwhile, it seems as though money is not a major problem. Money has allowed many bad causes to prolong the agony of death. Lack of funds has been blamed for the fall of organizations, corporations, governments, etc., but I really believe the fall of any organization or cause must go deeper than money.

It is encouraging to watch funds seem to appear out of nowhere just when they are needed the most. Several years ago Troop 9 needed new tents. The cost was going to be well over $600 (almost double that today). We wanted the boys to earn some of the money themselves so that they would appreciate and properly care for the tents when they were acquired, but we believed that we would have to somehow help them earn most of the required funds. One small notice was put in the church newsletter indicating our need for funds to purchase tents. The church had just hit the congregation, with only limited success, for money to purchase and pave a parking lot. The checks started to pour in. It was unbelievable. Without any hard sell or publicity, we soon had over $600, and had to return some of the checks that we didn't need.

The next year we decided we needed a trailer to haul the equipment. With very little effort a junk dealer sold us, for a token amount, the bed from an old plumber's truck, Sears donated tires, Firestone donated wheels, Wilson Hardware donated hasps and locks, and Quincy Technical School took on the refurbishing as a class project. We had a trailer for practically nothing.

The general public again came through for us last year. For several years, because of operating budget pressures, funds had not been made available to adequately maintain our local Scout reservation. The reservation was badly in need of repair. The idea of having a "Walk for Saukenauk" was copied from another council. During the initial planning, we believed we were very optimistic in setting a goal of $5,000. Within minutes of the first public news release, a local industry volunteered to match funds up to a maximum of $5,000 if the Scouts would do some good turn instead of just walking for money. With that incentive, a trash pick-up was incorporated into the walk plans. The day of the walk went well, with tons of trash collected in many communities in the council. But how much money would the boys collect from their sponsors?

The public response was astounding. The money collected for Saukenauk Scout Reservation maintenance was over $20,000. Any organization that is having trouble raising funds had better take a good, hard look in the mirror.

Why bother? You had better not ask me why I bother with Scouting unless you have all afternoon to kill.

Clyde Kangas

Photo Courtesy of Jim Boe

Chapter 6

Heartbreak Hill

Through absolutely no effort on my part, I was fortunate enough to be born into a home where I had a mother and father who loved me. They were wise enough to provide me with everything I needed, but not everything I wanted. They were foresighted enough to teach that both responsibility and hard work could be enjoyable. They complimented achievement, and offered encouragement in times of failure. They believed in stern discipline when deserved (which was rather frequently), and were certainly not overprotective.

It was only after I became a Scout leader as an adult that I woke up to the shocking fact that all boys do not have the privilege of growing up in the same kind of environment. I guess I assumed that all boys were fortunate enough to have a loving home environment.

There are many emotional times in the life of a Scoutmaster. Many such moments, as previously described, are humorous, rewarding, thankful, etc. There are also moments of sadness and anger. Usually these incidents are sorrow for the boy, and anger toward the parent for having created the particular situation. In general, I think of myself as a friendly, easygoing sort of guy who likes just about everyone. But I must admit that my fuse tends to get a little short when confronted with a situation where the parents obviously don't put the rearing of their own child on the very top of their personal priority list.

In the life of a Scout, probably his two proudest moments are when he receives his first recognition, the Scout badge (formerly the Tenderfoot badge), and when he receives the Eagle Scout badge, the highest honor which a Scout can achieve.

The Tenderfoot Investiture Ceremony, where the new Scout received his first badge, was traditionally an impressive candlelight ceremony which took place at a Court of Honor with all of the parents present. The new Tenderfoot Scouts were led forward in the darkened room and watched with beaming eyes as each of the twelve points of the Scout Law was explained, and the appropriate candle lit. They would then rededicate their belief in the Scout Oath by repeating it as the three candles representing duty to God and Country, duty to others, and duty to self, were lit by the Scoutmaster. The father was then called forward to pin the Tenderfoot badge on the uniform of his son. There were always smiles of pleasure and eager anticipation of Scouting events to come on the faces of the new Tenderfoot Scouts, all just eleven years old.

One father was a pillar of the community. He was an industrial leader of long standing in the city. He was a member of the governing body of his church. He was a member, chairman, or past president of many civic clubs, commissions, and councils in town. His picture was continually being recognized in the paper for his dedicated effort to serve his community or his industry. To say the least, he was a very busy man, well respected as a leader.

On one particular Wednesday night, he had two choices how he could spend his evening. He could clean up some paper work at his office in preparation for a business meeting the next day, or he could attend the Troop 9 Court of Honor where his son was to receive his Tenderfoot badge. Some cloth badge couldn't be as important as tomorrow's meeting, and anyway, he would be able to see his son and congratulate him the following morning at breakfast. He chose to go to his office.

That night I was filled with sadness and anger as I proudly pinned the Tenderfoot badge on that eleven year old's uniform, standing in for his father who was too busy to bother.

And then there was the weekend when our troop transportation chairman, George Elliott, was having trouble finding enough drivers to take us on a campout. One father, when asked, stammered and stuttered, and finally asked where we were going. When the reply was Saukenauk Scout Reservation, the father quickly, and with a relieved tone to his voice-said, "Oh, I can't drive. I never drive my car on gravel roads."

I certainly hope that the road to heaven is paved, for I wouldn't want this fellow to miss out on anything.

Death is difficult for everyone, regardless of the age of the deceased, but it seems even harder to accept when death comes to a youngster, who hasn't really had a chance to drink from the cup of life. Ten year old Scott Alberda was dying of leukemia. Ken, Scott's older brother, was a member of our troop, and Scott wanted also to be a Scout. It was difficult, but very rewarding to help a boy learn to tie a taut line hitch for his Tenderfoot requirements, knowing that he would probably not live to advance to the rank of Second Class. He was proud of mastering a knot, and eager to learn another, just as every other Scout whom I have helped with Scoutcraft skills. He was accepted at troop meetings and activities just as another member of the gang. No special privileges were extended, and none were requested by Scott.

I don't know why, but young boys seem to be able to accept death easier than adults. Several months later many of our Scouts were let out of school to attend Scott's funeral. While the boys were sorry to lose a friend, they seemed able to accept the fact that Scott would not be right here with us anymore, but life would go on anyway. They knew that it could have happened to any one of them but saw nothing to be benefited by worrying about it. They seemed to be able to handle the situation very well.

My Scouts all know that I am sort of a patriotic old cuss who still believes in respecting the American flag. It stands for our freedom. Many good men have given their lives so that we can live and worship in freedom under the flag of the United States of America.

Once in a while a show of temper can also be a valuable teaching tool. At the end of each troop meeting a patrol is assigned to put away all of the equipment and make sure the room is neat and orderly. The quality of this clean-up is pretty much in reverse relationship to the weather outside. Boys are more than glad to stay in and clean up if it is raining outside, but when the spring sun is out, the quality of the job can sometimes leave more than a little to be desired. For a couple of weeks I had noticed that the boys had been getting progressively sloppier in putting away the troop and American flags. Then after one meeting I found them just tossed in a corner of the closet. That was too much for this old flag waver to take. I began to set the stage for the following week's opening ceremony.

The next Wednesday night I arrived at the troop meeting room well in advance of the Scouts and removed the cast bronze eagle from the top of the flagpole so that it would not be broken. The Scouts soon arrived, and it was suggested that a circle be formed for the opening ceremony, which the Scouts conducted. After the opening, I took the flag and pole in my hands and quietly began telling a little of the history of our flag, with my voice building in volume and anger as I progressed. The boys all knew where they had left the flag following the previous meeting. The talk was ended by throwing the flag and pole into the middle of the ring of Scouts, angrily exclaiming, "If you don't think any more of your country's flag than you have demonstrated, why don't you take it out and stomp it into the mud!" Turning on my heels I left the room, leaving my Assistant Scoutmaster to oversee the remainder of the meeting.

I would definitely not recommend that the "blow your cool" routine be used very often, but it can be effective if there is a point that you really want to get across. I have never used it again. Also, it is not a good idea to discipline boys when you are really angry. It is much more effective and sets a better example if, whenever you are genuinely angry, to go off by yourself and kick a tree or something until you have regained your cool. People so often don't say what they mean and don't mean what they say in a fit of anger.

They boys displayed very good and very proper flag etiquette for the remainder of the Scouting year.

Another amusing incident, but with sad overtones, took place several years ago just after my wife returned from the hospital following a kidney operation. I was running late that evening, trying to fix dinner, do the dishes, get ready for Scout meeting, and serve as nurse all at the same time.

Like the television commercial, the telephone rang just when everything was not going smoothly. It was Dave, and he said he needed a ride to Scout meeting. I am a softy when it comes to providing rides to kids who need one, so said I would pick him up, even though it was clear across town.

When I got to his house, I saw his Dad's old truck parked in its usual place in front of the house. When Dave came out I asked him what was wrong with the truck. His reply was, "Nothing. I needed a ride because my Dad is taking a nap, and my Mom doesn't want to bother him."

On a recent canoe trip on the Current River in southern Missouri, we had just finished a full day on the water and had

Clyde Kangas

returned to our campsite for a good hot evening meal. In the name of expediency, we had canned beef stew to heat. It is a disgrace for any Scouter to admit to a menu such as heating a can or roasting a hot dog, but I guess we all fudge a little once in a while, rationalizing that we need the time for more important things. Now canned beef stew (if you can find the beef) is not exactly my idea of eating high on the hog, but at least we wouldn't starve.

Just as our gourmet chef was dumping it from can to pot, one of our newer boys exclaimed, "Don't forget to add three cans of water." The boy lived in a low income housing development with his parents and five brothers and sisters (with another in the hopper). Not until that camp-out, when he naturally wanted to water down the already watery beef stew like he did at home, did I realize what a hard time it must be trying to keep a family together without any money. The father was unemployed at the time.

It is a pleasure to see a family pull together like this one has done. While lack of money is a worry to the parents, it certainly hasn't hurt the family environment. They care about each other and work together as a team. Lack of funds has not impeded them from imparting good moral values to their children. They are too proud to accept charity and will undoubtedly rear better children because of their determined attitude and reluctance to sit back, curse their luck, and let the government support them. I would much rather have a son of mine grow up as a member of this family than as the son of the business leader who doesn't have time to bother with rearing his family.

I have not been able to find a common denominator that is characteristic of what I would consider "a good family environment." Neither wealth nor lack of it is common to the proper rearing of kids. Race and denomination of religion all seem to have their share of successes and failures. How would you rate your own home environment?

Never has my heart gone out to a boy as one December morning in 1972. It was the Monday morning between Christmas and New Year's, and I had to make a quick business trip to Denver. It is always crowded trying to travel during the holidays, but I had succeeded in getting a plane reservation.

Frontier Flight 7 from St. Louis to Denver was obviously going to be crowded. I was near the front of the line that Monday morning, thus got an aisle seat where I could have a little leg room. The plane was rapidly filling with families traveling over the holidays, a few vacationers heading for the ski slopes west of Denver, and a few businessmen like myself who couldn't postpone their trips until after the holidays.

Nearly all of the seats were taken, but the one right next to me was still open. A young boy of about twelve came up the aisle and asked if he could take that seat. Of course the answer was, "Yes." He was neatly dressed, very polite in his speech, and carrying a shiny new tape recorder with him, obviously a Christmas present.

Conversation soon started, and I learned that his name was Mark. From first observation, it appeared that Mark was the kind of boy who had everything going for him. From his ability to carry on a good conversation, it was apparent that he was no dummy. His clothes showed that he was not ready for the poor farm. His ability to travel alone with ease, indicated that he had a high level of self confidence. His polite manners indicated that he had received good training.

But before Frontier Flight 7 landed in Denver, two hours later. I had learned a lot more about young Mark that made me sick. Mark was on his way from spending Christmas with his mother in Missouri, to spend New Year's in Utah with his father.

Mark's parents had been divorced several years earlier. There had been an argument over who had to get stuck with Mark; not who got to keep Mark, but who got stuck with him. To solve the problem, Mark had been sent to a private boarding school during the winter and to private camps during the summer. Money was no object, so his parents saw to it that he was receiving the best of everything. The best schools, the best sports equipment, the best, the best, the best.

The private boarding school was closed this year over the Christmas and New Year's vacation, so the parents again compromised. Mom got stuck with Mark over Christmas and Dad over New Year's. This young boy was on his way this particular day from spending Christmas with a mother who didn't want him, to spend New Year's with a father who didn't want him. Mark had everything that money could buy, but he didn't have the love of a mother and father.

Many boys would have given up in such a situation, but I really believe that he had the strength and the courage to spit right in fate's eye, and make a go of it in spite of his parents. I didn't see Mark again after getting off that flight, but have often wondered how he is doing.

There are a lot of Marks in this world. Many live in a home where we assume love is present, but it really isn't. There is a good chance that there is a boy like Mark living within sight of your own home. We will never know unless we get involved with our youth. Kids the world over thirst for love and attention. They want someone to look up to, to admire, and in whose footsteps they can follow. Ideally this will be a parent, but will you be available when a parent drops the ball? A kid often puts up a fake front of not needing anybody; of being the tough guy who can stand on his own. But I have never seen an individual who did not respond positively to love, attention, and concern from another person.

Chapter 7

Close Calls

The statistical probability of accident or illness almost always increases for boys when they are engaged in Scouting activities. The activities are often in an environment that is foreign to the boy. They are often strenuous and tiring, creating fatigue by the end of the day. Food and water are usually different from what the boy is accustomed to eating and drinking. It is for these reasons that Scout leaders must take extra precautions to insure the health and safety of the boys in their charge.

Displacing a boy from the home environment of the Illinois Midwest to the high altitude mountains of Philmont, eating freeze-dried food for several days, and a tiring day on the trail with full pack, do increase the probability that he will burn himself while cooking supper.

The safety precautions taken by the Boy Scouts of America are, in my opinion, excellent. For water sports, the Eight Point Safe Swim Defense Plan has provided a safe swimming environment for many boys, regardless of their swimming ability. The merit badge program stresses safety, and first aid for illness and injury, should an accident occur. The attention given to health and safety at the summer camps and high adventure bases is outstanding. A boy is never intentionally placed in a situation which he is not physically capable of handling, but is provided the opportunity to experience adventures not ordinarily available to youth outside the Scouting program.

On various Scouting activities through the years, I have had my share of cuts, bruises, homesickness, etc., but have been indeed fortunate that no Scouts have been seriously injured.

When embarking on a two week—two thousand mile trip with a group of Scouts, a little prayer asking God's help in bringing the crew back safe and sound is always silently repeated. There seems to have been a giant protective hand watching over our crews.

There were three incidents that I would have to call close calls. A close call is a frightening experience, particularly when a parent had placed his son in your care and is depending on you to bring him back in one piece. After a close call, the thought each time crossed my mind, "Is it really worth it?" I could not get involved and not expose myself to the possibility of injuring or killing someone else's son. Why expose myself to the risk of liability? What would it be like to live with the knowledge that a boy in my care was permanently injured or killed? Why not let someone else shoulder the responsibility?

Each time the answer to these questions comes out the same. A boy can only grow through experiencing new challenges, meeting them head on, and conquering them. The more positive Christian influences to which a boy is exposed, the better are the odds that he will pass on the same positive example to the next generation. It was once said by someone, "Helping others is what the world is all about. A man might as well have never lived as to live without helping his fellow man." Yes, it is worth taking the risks. A close call is a reminder like a sledge hammer to the back of the head that the Scoutmaster can't afford to lose control of the situation, discipline must be enforced, safety precautions must be adhered to at all times, responsibility for the welfare of the group cannot be delegated.

One warm spring weekend I was canoeing the Current River in Southern Missouri from Round Spring to Powder Mill Ferry with several Scouts. To break the routine of paddling, we decided to scale one of the high bluffs that overlooks the river in many places. We were certain that the view from the top would be worth the climb.

The particular bluff that we chose appeared to be steep enough to be a challenge, but not so steep that it would be dangerous to a group of novice campers without any equipment. I was in the lead, with a couple of the boys right behind me. The climb was proving to be easier than initially anticipated. Suddenly a rock gave way beneath my foot and went hurtling down the side of the hill, missing Doug Hunt's head by only inches. The incident was over almost before it began. No one was injured, not a word was said, and we proceeded to the summit of the bluff without another incident.

It was a cold but sunny winter Saturday afternoon in Michigan. Five inches of fluffy new snow had fallen the night before, making the snowmobile trails along Lake Michigan just about perfect. One of my Scouts was riding shotgun on the back of my snowmobile. We had been riding in and out, up and down the sand dunes along the lake, often retreating to the beauty of the snow covered pine tree forests inland several blocks from the shoreline. What a great day to be alive and enjoying the beauties of nature.

We took a break with a thermos of hot chocolate along North Shore Road where my car and snowmobile trailer were parked. The boy with me was very conscientious and responsible, so I told him to take the machine out for a spin by himself. After watching him skillfully handle the snowmobile for about five minutes, I saw him head toward the road. There was a car coming down the icy road, which was blocked from his view by another parked vehicle. With that sinking feeling of horror, it appeared to me that a collision was inevitable. That split second seemed like an hour while I waited for the car to skid, the sound of the crash, and the sight of Dave being thrown through the air. It didn't happen. The car kept going, there was no crash, and my snowmobile was still hidden from view by the parked car. When I got to the machine, the front skis had hit a patch of dry asphalt, bringing it to an abrupt halt, just short of the roadway. That was the only patch of dry asphalt that I could see in either direction. Was that luck? Don't you believe it for a minute. I don't believe that Dave ever realized what a close call he had.

The third and final close call was pure negligence on my part. It was a warm spring Saturday afternoon. I was camping with Troop 5 along the banks of the Little Muskegon River in Michigan. It was the first really warm weekend after a long and cold winter. The boys were overly anxious to go swimming in the river. We looked along the bank for a place that could be used with a relatively high degree of safety. About a mile upstream we found a swimming hole that had a rope swing on an overhanging branch of a cedar tree. It was obviously a favorite swimming hole for the local neighborhood boys.

The bottom was checked, buddies were assigned, and soon we were ready to hit the water, of course, after posting a lifeguard. But I neglected to check the swimming ability of all of the boys. I knew that all but our two newest Scouts were good swimmers. One of the new boys said he couldn't swim, and I assumed that the other could. That proved to be a bad assumption. When it came his turn to swing out over the water and drop, he attacked the rope swing with all the enthusiasm of an Olympic swimmer, but when he hit the water, it was immediately obvious that he couldn't swim a lick. We had Mike out of the water and on the bank within seconds, very scared, but unhurt.

The most serious actual injury occurred while on a Scouting activity as we were preparing to canoe the Big Piney River near Fort Leonard Wood, Missouri. We had been guests of the United States Army at Fort Leonard Wood the previous night. We had invited our escort officer to accompany us on our float trip. Just as we were preparing to start the float, our escort officer (I don't even remember his name) slammed a car door on his thumb. At the sight of his own blood, he started to pass out. Dr. Don Sandercock, our dentist, medical advisor, parent, and assistant scoutmaster, did the first aid honors before we delivered our battle scarred lieutenant back to the Army.

There was only one occasion when the old Scoutmaster required medical attention. While taking a night hike at Gerber Scout Reservation, I somehow managed to jab my eye with the branch of a tree. I guess I thought if I ignored the problem, it would go away. The eye kept me awake half the night, and by morning I knew medical attention would be required to remove the boulder, log, elephant, or whatever it was that was still in my eye.

Whitehall was the nearest town with a doctor. I knew the doctor would be overjoyed about coming out on a Sunday morning. I called him from a service station, and he directed me to his home. He soon had me patched up good as new. When he saw my Scout uniform he refused to take any pay, indicating that he was a day or two behind on his good turns, and perhaps this would help him catch up.

Challenge and a degree of danger often seem to go hand in hand. There have been times when I have placed boys (and myself intentionally in a small degree of danger in an attempt to force meeting a challenge. For several New Year's weekends I have taken senior Scouts canoeing on the Current River in Missouri. Canoeing several miles from the nearest assistance, in icy water and below freezing temperatures, certainly is not the safest thing to do, but has provided many enjoyable weekends. Canoes have capsized a couple times, but the teamwork getting a fire started, clothes dry, etc., had been sensational. When they have to, boys always seem to come through like troopers.

Only once on these Polar Bear canoe trips did we meet a fellow crazier than we. Upon rounding a bend in the river near Akers Ferry, there was a man clad only in his skivies and a tee shirt, standing knee deep in the icy water, with a mirror in one hand, a razor in the other, and a face covered with lather. After exchanging pleasantries, he indicated his disappointment that it wasn't snowing. We later found that he was a member of a canoe club that takes a float trip on the Current River every New Year's Day.

Photo Courtesy of Jim Boeger

Chapter 8
Accepted As Something Special

The purpose of wearing a uniform is to present an image to the public. That image is often different to different people. To the average law-abiding citizen, the uniform of a police officer presents the image of a friend to whom we can turn when assistance is needed. The person in the police uniform is expected to defend our life and property. To the bank robber, the same uniform represents an enemy. Regardless of where we are in these United States, we all have an image in our minds whenever we see the police officer. We automatically expect something of the uniform, regardless of who is behind the uniform—black or white, Yank or Confederate, fat or thin, Protestant or Jew. Think about it for a minute. We automatically associate certain expectations from people, with the uniform that they are wearing.

The uniform of the Boy Scouts of America is also associated with certain expectations. Usually the Scout uniform is associated with good. Once in a while a person will have a different opinion, but it is the exception.

In traveling across America, it is interesting to note the difference in the reception that I receive depending on whether I am traveling on vacation or business as an ordinary citizen, or whether I am traveling with Scouts in a Scout uniform.

The general public seems to expect a well-behaved, honest, and dependable behavior pattern from a boy wearing the

Scout uniform. People also expect Scout groups to be under good and disciplined leadership. When traveling with Scouts it is enjoyable to have complete strangers come up and introduce themselves. Most relate the uniform with pleasing experiences from their boyhood days, or relate the uniform to their own hometown Scouting experiences, often that of a parent or Scout leader. They seem to know that a Scouter won't be offended by a stranger introducing himself. All seem more than willing to offer any assistance that may be needed.

Traveling across the country with Scout groups readily impresses one with the very favorable image that the Scout uniform has in the eyes of the general public. It is a real challenge to try to live up to that image. One cannot help but be concerned to see that his particular group does nothing to tarnish that image.

There have been frequent occasions when strangers have come over to our table in a public restaurant just to thank us for being Scout leaders, and giving boys the opportunity to see more of our great country, whether it be near the Boundary Waters Canoe Area at Ely, Minnesota, in one of the small Kansas towns on the way to Philmont, or in downtown St. Louis in the shadow of the Gateway Arch. After attending church services in Wausau, Wisconsin, on our way to Northern Wisconsin National Canoe Base, we received an invitation to lunch for our crew of twelve from a stranger in the congregation. It almost seems that a Scout uniform is never among strangers.

I have never had a church door closed to our traveling Scout groups. U. S. military bases have been more than cooperative in providing food and lodging for our troop. Below are listed several experiences which indeed make me proud to wear my Scout uniform anywhere, anytime.

It was the Saturday just before Memorial Day weekend. Our troop had just completed hiking the Piasa Bird Trail, located between Alton and Grafton, Illinois. The 14 mile hike had given us our exercise for the day, through one of the prettiest parts of the Mississippi River valley.

It had been a good day. The morning started out warm and sunny. The Piasa Bird Trail Committee representative had given us a warm reception and had thanked us for hiking their trail. The boys had all enjoyed the hike, with only a few minor blisters giving a problem to a couple of our Tenderfoot Scouts.

It was about 4:00 P.M. and had started to drizzle on us the last mile of the hike. We covered that last mile in record time to seek the shelter of our cars. We had had a late lunch, so agreed to drive straight through to Quincy, not attempting to stay together, but planning to take the boys on to their individual homes. I was last in line pulling out of the parking lot.

Down the road about a mile, one of the Scouts sitting in the back yelled, "The car is on fire!" A quick check of the gauges on the instrument panel showed no problem, and I didn't smell any smoke, but a quick glance in the rear view mirror revealed a cloud behind us. Obviously it was steam and not smoke.

The other cars in our group had disappeared ahead of us in the rain. Obviously there was no way to get assistance from them. A quick check under the hood revealed that a freeze plug had blown out of the engine block, draining all of the water. The Mississippi River was only a few feet away on the right side of the highway, so I tried pouring a bucket of river water into the radiator, but it ran out as fast as I could pour it in. Obviously I wasn't going anywhere. A tow truck would be needed to haul my car into a garage where a mechanic was on duty. It was really raining hard now.

For several minutes I tried thumbing a ride, after having told the boys to stay in the car. Cars continued to whiz past. It was obvious that people weren't about to stop to pick up a big guy like me in a downpour. I was wearing a black rain suit with an old grubby hat and probably looked like a pretty desperate character. I kept thinking, "Would I pick up a stranger on the highway on a day like this?" My answer to myself was, "No." But I would pick up a man in a Scout uniform. In spite of the rain I took off my rain coat so that my Scout uniform was showing. Within seconds, both of the next two cars pulled over and stopped.

Thanks to the Scout uniform, it was less than an hour until we were again on our way home with a new freeze plug in place. In that hour I received a ride to the nearest town, obtained a tow truck, to haul us back to Alton, and persuaded a mechanic to leave his supper and open his garage to get us back on the road. John Doe citizen may well have had to wait until the following Monday morning to get the trouble repaired.

People seem to know that a man wearing a Scout uniform is where he is because he wants to help boys, not for his own personal gain, etc. People seem more than happy to do their best to help any traveling Scout group.

A fellow Scouter, Harold Hillebrenner, tells the story that happened to one of his four sons a few years ago. Young Hillebrenner received his Eagle Scout Award in Troop 45 sponsored by Salem Evangelical United Church of Christ in

Quincy, Illinois. He graduated from high school and went on to college in Utah. Toward the end of his senior year, he started to run a little short of cash. Of course, he knew that he could write back home and ask Dad for more money, but he was too proud to do that except as a last resort. He just needed about a hundred dollars to finish his college education.

Banks are in the business of loaning money, so it was an obvious place to go. Not being bashful, he made an appointment to see the President of the local bank. Things went fine until the banker asked about collateral to guarantee the loan. Now what kind of collateral could a college senior possibly have? No car, no job yet; he wouldn't need the loan if he had enough money to afford what the bank considered collateral.

Dejected, he started to leave the bank without the loan. Dad would send the money if asked, but surely there was another way. Just as he reached the door at the front of the bank, he remembered a wrinkled card which he carried in his billfold. He walked back into the banker's office and thrust forward his Eagle Scout card. "Is this good enough collateral?" he asked. A smile came on the banker's face as he replied, "No, son, it isn't good enough for this bank, but it is for me." With that the banker wrote young Mr. Hillebrenner his personal check for one hundred dollars.

That banker wasn't trusting my friend's son with his money, he was trusting an Eagle Scout with his money. It could have been any Eagle Scout. This is the image that is expected of every Eagle Scout.

There have been times when the generosity and hospitality of fine people is so overwhelming that it is almost embarassing. When you have said thanks twenty times and still more kindnesses are being thrust upon you, it really gives one a warm feeling about the friendliness of one's fellowman. Such was the case one August in Minneapolis as we were on our way to canoe in the Boundary Waters Canoe Area north of Ely with Troop 9.

The year before we had read in the paper that a troop from Minneapolis was coming down the Mississippi by outboard boat, headed for Hannibal, Missouri. Wanting to extend the warm hand of Scouting friendship, we drove north that evening to Canton, Missouri, and passed the evening around the campfire with the Minnesota Scouts. They were outfitted with about a dozen new boats and outboard motors that had been loaned by the manufacturer for the trip. An American flag was flown from an improvised mast on each boat. This was really a sharp looking crew, with obviously excellent leadership. The following evening we again met them at Hannibal, the termination of their trip. We really didn't do anything for them except offer assistance if it was needed.

The following year when our troop decided to go north for a week of canoeing, I wrote their Scoutmaster asking if we could bed down in their church basement on our way through Minneapolis. Of course the answer was, "Yes."

When we arrived on a warm August afternoon, there was Bob Lee, their Scoutmaster, waiting for us at their church. A wash tub of ice cold soda awaited us in the basement. Did that ever taste good after being behind the wheel all day!

After driving all day, we weren't really ready to hit the night life of greater Minneapolis with ten wild and wooly Scouts, so were more than eager to accept Scoutmaster Lee's invitation to see movies of their Mississippi River trip the year before. After seeing their films, it was obvious that their troop had had an educational and heart warming experience. It appeared that they had been warmly received at every town where they stopped, from Minneapolis to Hannibal.

We thanked them for showing us their movies, and were just about ready to sack out for the night when their committee chairman indicated that some of the mothers had refreshments waiting for our boys in the kitchen. Sure enough, there were most of their Scout Troop and parents with more homemade blueberry pies than I had seen in one place in a long time. We were almost overwhelmed by their friendly hospitality.

Before leaving, a couple members of their troop committee asked when we would be leaving the following morning. I indicated that we wanted to get an early start, so would probably get up about 5:30 A.M., and planned to be on the road by 6:00 A.M. That seemed to be satisfactory. We again thanked our hosts and retired for the night.

The next morning I awoke to the sound of bells. It soon dawned on me that it was the sound of my alarm clock, for 5:30 A.M. had arrived already. Amid some grumbles and groans, the lights were turned on, and the solid sea of sleeping bags on the floor started to wiggle and squirm. There was soon a flurry of action stuffing stuff into packs, getting shirts on right side out, rolling up sleeping bags and air mattresses, etc.

My first venture out of the room a few minutes later revealed a light at the end of the hall about where I remembered the kitchen to be. That was funny, for I was sure that we had turned out all of the lights before retiring the night before. Investigation showed several of the adults from their troop committee busy fixing breakfast for us. Fantastic! I don't know what time those men had to get up to get breakfast going by 5:30 A.M.

Several members of their troop committee indicated that other Scout troops, churches, and individuals had done many favors for them the previous year on their Mississippi River trip, and there was no way that they could repay all of those favors, but they could show kind hospitality to any troops needing assistance while passing through the Minneapolis area. I am confident that it will be a long time before our Scouts and leaders forget the good turn performed for us on that trip through Minneapolis. A friendly good turn like that can and does often leave a permanent and very positive mark on the character of a boy.

There were a couple of times when our reception was not quite so friendly. On the way home on the same trip, we stopped in Virginia, Minnesota, for two reasons: to eat dinner, and to visit one of the large open pit iron mines. After supper at one of the local restaurants, a couple of the younger Scouts wanted to walk around the block, just to stretch their legs, I guess. We were a little ahead of schedule, so had no objections.

A few minutes later they came running back into the restaurant in a flurry of excitement. It seems that a drunk was staggering down the street, took a swing at Kevin, and knocked him down. Fortunately he was more scared than hurt.

Two days later when we got home, the first thing that Kevin said when his parents came to the church to pick him up was, "Guess what! I got beat up by an old drunk." I looked around for a rock to hide under, but none was big enough. I could just guess what was going through his Mom's mind after a greeting like that. Evidently they didn't think that our leadership was too untrustworthy, for their second son joined our troop just this fall. That proved to be another incident that made an impression on the boy's minds, for "the day Kevin got slugged by a drunk," is still retold on frequent occasions around the campfire.

The only other cool reception that I can remember receiving was last summer on the way to Philmont. We stopped for lunch at a truck stop and restaurant in western Kansas. Our dozen Scouts were all in proper uniform and looked pretty sharp, if I do say so myself. There wasn't a table large enough for our whole crew, so we split up at three different tables.

We greeted the waitress with a friendly, "Hi, how are you today?" The short reply, "Well, I was fine till you all came in." We weren't sure whether she was joking or serious right at first, but after not getting even a glass of water in the next five minutes, we concluded that she was serious; we made our exit and had a very enjoyable lunch about a block down the street.

There are only a few major events in recent history that were significant enough that most people can remember where they were and what they were doing when "it" happened. One such event was the unfortunate assassination of President Kennedy. Another such event was the night man first walked on the moon.

For almost a year, our troop had been scheduled to start a week of summer camp on this particular Sunday July afternoon at Grand Valley Scout Reservation in central Michigan. We had been following the progress of the space flight for several days, and knew that the moon landing and first step on the moon would take place sometime that evening, when we were far from civilization.

It was the first year that Grand Valley Scout Reservation was open, thus the facilities were still very primitive. There was an administration building, but no structure nearly large enough to hold all of the campers. We resigned ourselves to reading about the moon landing the following week when we got back home and could dig up a newspaper. It was too bad that Scouts would have to miss such an historic event, but we really didn't see any alternative.

I guess some of the local residents also thought that boys should not miss seeing such an historic event. After supper several people appeared with television sets under their arms. The sets were positioned in the windows of the administration building, facing outward. Word spread like wildfire, and soon the building was surrounded with boys and leaders listening to Walter Cronkite narrate the events as they were taking place on the surface of the moon.

It was hot that night. The reservation was surrounded by a swampy marsh, thus the mosquitoes were terrible. We were all swatting ourselves and the person in front of us. It was a mass cooperative effort to try to keep the mosquitoes from eating us alive. Then that first step was taken, and a cheer went up from our group. We could endure the mosquitoes no longer, and within a few seconds everyone had scurried to the safety of the mosquitoe netting in their tents.

Thanks to the thoughtful generousity of a few neighbors, over a hundred boys were able to watch mankind take his first step in pioneering outer space. Thank goodness for neighbors like this who believe in being good neighbors and in the program of the Boy Scouts of America.

Sometimes boys are self-conscious about wearing the Scout uniform; especially the older Scouts. I guess they don't want to be singled out as a kid in a green suit. Perhaps they think other peers will consider them sissies. Quite frankly I am proud to wear the uniform and have attempted to convey that pride to Scouts.

Occasionally when traveling, I have set a day aside when we will not wear our uniforms. It is soon obvious that doors are not as easily opened; receptions are not always as friendly. The uniform of the Boy Scouts of America is truly "accepted as something special."

Clyde Kangas

Photo Courtesy of Jim Boeger

Chapter 9
High Adventure

High adventure is to Scouting what icing is to a cake. It's fun. It's exciting. It's a challenge.

As previously stated, a first Polar Bear Camporee is looked forward to with enthusiasm. It is a new experience trying not only to survive, but to survive in relative comfort in subfreezing and snowy conditions. The first time is a challenge. It is easy to get in a rut where the fifth or sixth Polar Bear Camporee is looked forward to as just another cold camp-out. Such is not the case with the high adventure bases of the Boy Scouts of America. They never seem to get to be routine. There is always something different over the next mountain or around the next bend in the river. I have always looked forward to taking my next high adventure trip with excitement and enthusiasm. Five consecutive years of taking high adventure expeditions, and I am ready for another five at least.

The spirit of teamwork is probably the biggest lesson to be learned by crews taking part in a high adventure expedition, be it at Philmont, Land Between the Lakes, Northern Wisconsin National Canoe Base, Charles Sommers Wilderness Canoe Base, or any of the other high adventure bases administered by the Boy Scouts of America.

The first day out the crews typically are unorganized, a little confused, reluctant to lend a hand unless ordered to do so, etc. It is a pleasure to watch these same boys develop into an organized team within a few days. After that spirit of teamwork has effectively been accomplished, the job of the adult leader really becomes a pleasure. Hiking down Tooth Ridge into tent city after ten days at Philmont, or paddling across White Sand Lake after a week at Northern Wisconsin National Canoe Base (formerly Region Seven Canoe Base), there seems to be real pride just radiating from a good crew. They have spent days in the wilderness having to depend on each other. They have knit together to form a team. They feel as though they could conquer any empire, climb any mountain, swim any ocean. There is a real feeling of pride being a member of such a well coordinated team—a feeling that is not often experienced. Some people never have the opportunity, in a whole lifetime, to be a member of such a team.

Only one high adventure crew, of which I was a leader, failed, at least in my opinion, to develop that esprit de corps of being a team, the feeling of closeness that we could handle any challenge that came our way, that feeling of knowing one could rely on any other member of the crew. I almost sensed that few wanted to do more than absolutely necessary to get by. In every crew there are those who can't, or won't, pull their fair share of the load. For teamwork to really develop, there must also be those willing to pick up the slack. This is true not just of a high adventure crew, but of life in general. The difference between a successful leader and a routine follower is the willingness to tackle a challenge head on, and stick to the task in spite of cumbersome roadblocks.

Why did we not develop strong team spirit on that particular expedition? None of our Scouts that trip had ever had to worry about where the next meal was coming from. In fact, many haven't even had to worry about where the next Cadillac was coming from. Perhaps we have made it too easy on our younger generation. Perhaps we have tried to give them too much rather than letting them learn the hard way. Perhaps we just failed as leaders in our attempt to develop this teamwork. Perhaps it would have developed had we had a few more days together. Perhaps it was really there and we just didn't recognize it. Perhaps we just expected too much from our fine crew that year. Whatever the reason, I can't put my finger on why I believe the team spirit never developed to its full potential with that crew. But of this I am sure; any boy who has the false impression that he can mature into a happy and successful adult without doing more than just his job; by doing just enough to get by, is in for some disappointing years.

The remainder of this chapter is a diary of one of my recent Philmont expeditions. Depicted will be some of the joys and frustrations of being mother, father, teacher, minister, chauffeur, and policeman, for a dozen young men for a couple of weeks. Events from other high adventure expeditions will be interspersed in the narrative where appropriate.

Philmont Minus 10 Months

Philmont! This was the day that I took the final plunge and mailed the reservation check to Philmont Scout Ranch near Cimarron, New Mexico. Since returning from Philmont two years earlier, I had been convinced that I would return but was unsure which year. All this past summer I had been toying with the idea of returning again next summer. Memories included the never ending rain, crawling into a sleeping bag after going three days without a shower, eleven days on the trail with only one change of socks, that feeling down in the pit of your stomach when you hear a noise outside the tent, after hearing of all the damage a bear had done the night before, trying to start a fire for breakfast after a rain that would float Noah's ark, and listening to ten young men squabble over why they shouldn't have to wash dishes. In spite of these, Philmont, to me, is like a magic magnet that is always calling. At work, on a plane, in church, around the campfire; many times each year the pull of the invisible Philmont magnet can be felt. It is a place of natural and unspoiled beauty. It is a place where news, television, newspapers, radio, telephones, and other pressures of our hum drum routine world are completely foreign and pushed far back into the recesses of our minds. It is a place where many boys prove to themselves that they are men.

The date requested, when mailing in the reservation check, would enable us, hopefully, to miss the late July monsoon season. Getting our reservation request in that early should enable us to obtain the requested early August arrival date at Philmont.

There was still plenty of time to announce the trip to Troop 9, for I was certain that we would have no trouble filling the contingent.

Philmont Minus 8 Months

Earlier in the week the monthly troop newsletter to parents told of the Philmont plans, and that reservations would be accepted on a first come—first served basis. Almost immediately several Scouts called and made their reservations. By ten minutes before the start of our Wednesday night troop meeting, the crew quota of ten boys and two leaders was filled with deposits paid, or a promise that, "Mom will bring the check after the meeting." Two of our older Scouts came to the meeting a few minutes late with reservation checks in hand. I was sorry that we had to turn them down, and they were equally disappointed. They were given the name of another Scoutmaster who still had a few vacancies.

Frankly I don't believe that most of the Scouts really knew what Philmont was all about but had been caught up in the enthusiasm from hearing about others' experiences. I was confident that none would be disappointed.

Bill Rummenie had agreed to be the second adult advisor. I was glad to have Bill, for he loved to hike and camp, had been to Philmont twice previously, worked well as Assistant Scoutmaster of Troop 9, and just might be able to outhike me if he really set his mind to it. All of the Scouts in the crew were long time members of Troop 9, and, except for a transfer, had been with our troop since receiving their Tenderfoot badges three or four years before.

Philmont Minus 4 Months

This was the organizational meeting for Scouts and parents. Slides from Bill Rummenie's previous Philmont expeditions were shown, the itinerary was explained and reviewed, an equipment list was reviewed, health and safety rules were reviewed, and a variety of questions were answered once, twice, and sometimes three times.

When bears, rock slides, and flash floods were discussed back to back, I thought we were going to lose Diane Kirsch, one of the worried moms, from our midst, but she managed to hang in there with her fingers and toes crossed.

Bill and I had chosen the itinerary, primarily because we knew the country, and knew what parts of Philmont we thought the boys would enjoy. Bill had been to the North Country, with it s dry, rugged canyons and ridges, on both of his previous trips. I had been to the South Country with its pine forests and grassy meadows. We compromised, and chose an itinerary that started in the wooded mountains and meadows of the South Country, and worked north almost the full length of the ranch, ending near Baldy Mountain at the northwest corner of the ranch.

Undoubtedly our enthusiasm for Philmont spilled over to some of the boys. It was obvious from the questions that some had reservations about leaving a warm, comfortable home for a place with bears, mud, lightning, rocks under your sleeping bag, and no television, but none openly voiced their doubts.

The crew leader for the expedition was elected. The duty roster for the other camp chores was explained and assigned in short order. On the whole, it looked like we were going to have a good crew. Half of the Scouts had been with us the previous year at Northern Wisconsin National Canoe Base for a week long canoe trip. Others had been to the National Jamboree in Idaho. All knew how to camp, and all had worked together in the troop. It was obvious that some were not in the best of physical condition, thanks to television, spectator sports, and the "good life." However, being able to endure the physical hardships of a Philmont expedition is more a state of mind than pure physical strength. I have seen boys small in size make it with ease over those mountains, primarily because of their determination that they could do it, and nothing was going to stop them from enjoying the high country to its fullest. I have seen others much bigger and much stronger who had to be driven back to base camp, simply because they lacked confidence in themselves that they could meet the challenge. Those who don't make it are the exceptions.

After the night's orientation session, I was ready to head west. Four months seemed like a long time to have to wait.

It is sometimes said that 60% of the enjoyment of a high adventure expedition is in the pre-planning, another 60% is in reliving the memories after the expedition is over, and the actual enduring of the trip counts as a negative 20%. I don't know how correct the percentages are, but I do know that I anxiously look forward to these trips each summer.

Philmont Minus 2 Months

It was the day for taking a shakedown hike, primarily to get the boys accustomed to the feel of a pack on their backs, give them an idea of their physical condition, and to again review what to and what not to take along with them. Each Scout was to bring his pack with 35 pounds of weight. This would be the average pack weight while on the trail.

As we loaded the cars, many of the packs were obviously fresh off the store shelf. These boys would soon discover that putting a pack on one's back to get the feel of it and lugging it over five miles of hills were two entirely different things.

We headed for Wildwood Girl Scout Center, about 35 miles east of Quincy, for the shakedown. It was a beautiful day, with the temperature just about right for some strenuous exercise. We started at a slow pace along one of the marked trails. About a mile out, we went through a nice, big, lush, poison ivy patch. In another mile Randy tripped over something, and ended up tail over tea kettle in a ditch. About that time Mr. Rummenie took over the lead from me. Our fearless leader gallantly blazed the trail—right into a big patch of black fireweed. There wasn't any place to go but right through it. Tim and I were wearing long pants, so were begged to take the lead, at least until we got out of the fireweed. Even the long pants didn't help that much. We all itched like the devil. At the next stream, we stopped to wash off as much of the stuff as possible.

We trucked on for about five miles before ending back at the Parker Hilton (Wildwood Administration Building) where we joined a Girl Scout troop and a work crew for a sack lunch. It was a good day just to lie back and fall asleep under an old shade tree. The big attraction after lunch was that somebody discovered a dead rabbit in the root cellar behind the Parker Hilton. Poking around at the dead rabbit seemed to keep the kids occupied for half an hour. After that we set up the tents which some of the boys were planning to take. They looked good and were all approved for use at Philmont. We neglected to check to see that all the boys had used the bottle of seam waterproofing that came with their tents. Apparently some of the boys didn't know why they had gotten a bottle of waterproofing with their new tent, thus had thrown it away. This we did not discover until several months later at Clarks Fork Camp.

Then it was time to see which boys could really hack it. We hiked to the bottom of Wildwood's steepest hill. When at the bottom, we announced a race to the top, with full pack. Somehow I managed to outpace the kids, with Ben and Bill Rummenie right behind. Ben was obviously in the best physical condition of any of the Scouts. Most finished shortly, even though they were huffing and puffing pretty hard. There were a couple that came in really dragging, who obviously had to get into better physical condition before Philmont, or have a miserable time trying to keep up with the rest of the group.

No comment was made regarding the physical condition of any Scout, for it was obvious to each what his own condition was. Mike moaned and groaned about how he was about to croak. I really believe he should have won an Academy Award for that performance, for he appeared to be in pretty good shape to me.

Philmont—Day 1

The day was finally here. It was a Saturday morning early in August, and we were ready to head west for Philmont. My travelall was washed, my list was checked and double checked, the money was all in—what had I forgotten? Everyone was early at the church for a change, and we were all ready to go. Oops, Randy forgot his sack lunch, so his dad made a mad dash some place to get a lunch. The boys looked sharp in their uniforms, freshly pressed and clean. A few pictures were taken, Randy's Dad dashed up with his lunch, and we were again ready to go, almost on time.

We didn't even get out of the parking lot until forgetful John remembered that he had forgotten his hiking boots, and thought they were in his mom's car. Now if he could just remember where her car was supposed to be. We agreed to catch up with Bill Rummenie west of Hannibal while we went in search of John's boots. We drove across town to his home, but no car. Just as we turned the corner, she came driving up the street. Fifteen minutes late, we were finally heading across the Mississippi River for two weeks of mountain adventure.

We hoped that the first hour wasn't a forecast of what was to come, for we started in the rain. We overtook Bill and his car load of wild Indians west of Hannibal, and pushed westward the rest of the morning. At the first gas stop, those who hadn't ridden with Bill before learned the rules—no food or drink in the car. With long faces, a couple of boys pitched their half drunk soda cans in the trash, and climbed aboard just as we pulled out. The boys traded cars frequently. They all knew that Bill's car had a radio, but that they could get away with more horse play when riding with me. They still haven't found any way to get the best of both worlds.

We stopped for lunch just north of Kansas City at a roadside park. We descended like an invading army on one of the picnic shelters. Within minutes, we had the whole shelter to ourselves. I couldn't imagine why the other people moved to another vacant shelter!

On the way across Missouri there was more poking, jabbing, punching, tickling, and giggling than one would expect from a whole bus load of eight year old girls. Once John was leaning over the front seat trying to grab a back seat occupant when someone gave him a good goose right where it counts. John straightened up so fast that he slammed his head into the roof of the travelall. Unfortunately that only slowed him down for about five minutes.

We arrived at the Harry S. Truman Museum and Library in Independence, Missouri, shortly after lunch. Our older Scouts charged in under a full head of steam and disappeared. Before Bill and I could orient our map to see which room we were in, they were back saying, "We've seen it all, let's go." They seemed totally uninterested in looking at a bunch of old historical junk. The younger members of the crew took their time, looked at most of the exhibits, and seemed genuinely interested in learning a little more about the history of our great country.

Shortly we were headed west across Kansas for Fort Riley, where we would spend the first night, guests of the U. S. Army.

We passed the time trying to guess how many miles it was to a distant hill on the horizon. When that wore off, they played Spud. The first person to spot a Volkswagen bug would yell Spud. My ears are still ringing from the sound of five boys all yelling Spud at the same time, and then arguing over who yelled it first.

We arrived at Fort Riley about an hour ahead of schedule, and waited on the lawn for our escort officer to pick us up. Mike learned the hard way what happens when anyone gives Mr. Rummenie a rough time after a hard day's drive.

Our escort officer turned out to be a polite new recruit who didn't know where anything was located. With some help, he managed to get us to our barracks and to the mess hall. All day Bill and I had been filling our boys with bull about how every Army post in the world always serves liver every Saturday night. We had them all primed into having to choke down liver for supper. They were pleasantly surprised at having a choice of ham hocks and beans or hamburgers. We mumbled something about the new Army having changed a lot.

After supper we went swimming in one of the post pools. I went into town for some ice cream while the rest of the crew was in the pool. Everyone appeared to be in pretty good shape after the first day.

When the pool closed, there was still some daylight left. We went in search of the obstacle course (which we probably weren't supposed to do). After a couple of miles of hiking, we found it. We tried part of it, but I drew the line when some wanted to climb the parachute tower.

We really appreciate the facilities that are made available to visiting Scout troops by military installations. A warm bed, a hot shower, and good food, at almost no cost, helps to make such a trip a little easier both on the leader and on the budget. The Army generally does an excellent job of hosting visiting Scouts.

Our crew leader led us in a worship service before we turned in for the night. This was just another example of how a small, private service such as we had there in the barracks, can be more meaningful than attending services in a large cathedral. We had quite a variety of denominations represented in our crew, with Catholic, Jewish, and four denominations of Protestants.

When we were almost asleep, another troop came in, who were to sleep in the second floor of the barracks. They were under excellent leadership. That leader kept them quiet and had them bedded down in a matter of minutes. It is surely easy to tell which groups are under good leadership. I honestly believe that the groups that are under good leadership and strong discipline have more fun than those that are allowed to run wild.

Philmont—Day 2

We were up before dawn, hoping to get most of Kansas behind us before the late afternoon sun completely cooked us. We tried to make as little noise as possible, so as not to awaken the troop sleeping upstairs. We drove three hours before stopping in Great Bend for breakfast. The town seemed to be just starting to wake up. The food was good, and the price was right, the restaurant was very nice, and our boys were on their best behavior. It is a pleasure to be the leader of a group of Scouts like ours.

When passing through one town, Bill pulled up beside a pick-up truck at a stop light. There was a big dog in the back of the truck, and a shapely blonde riding shotgun in the front. Tom exclaimed in his usual quiet voice, "Did you see that dog!" Bill answered back, equally quietly, "That doesn't look like any dog to me." With that Bill got a smile and a wink as the truck took off in a cloud of dust.

Mile after mile of harvested wheat fields, rolling prairie hills, feeder cattle lots, and oil wells passed by the rest of the morning. Many of our crew had not seen the prairies of Kansas before. Fortunately the temperature was below the normal August highs. It wasn't cool, but bearable.

For excitement we ate lunch at a Pizza Hut, crossed into Colorado, and entered the Mountain Time Zone. No one argued when given instructions to have a sandwich, and no pizza for lunch. Perhaps our preaching about balanced diet had sunk in just a little. Nobody complained about having to stay in the cars so long, for we all knew this was necessary to get to Philmont. We were aware that we were steadily climbing in elevation, and soon passed a sign saying that we were at 3,000 ft.

By mid afternoon we had arrived at the Koshare Indian Kiva in LaJunta, Colorado, where we would spend the night as guests of the Koshare Indian Dancers. We gave the crew a few minutes to unwind, buy gifts, see the Koshare Indian art collection, and Indian artifacts museum. The collection that has been acquired by the Koshares over the years is priceless. They are really doing a great job of preserving some of the Indian culture for future generations. The Koshares did not have a performance scheduled for the evening, but we did get to see the costumes that they wear for their dances.

We soon headed for the municipal swimming pool to cool off

the troops. There was an A & W right across the street. We kept a sharp eye on Tom to see that he didn't drink himself sick. He seemed to be eating everything in sight at every stop. We soon adopted the name Garbage Head for Tom. He lived up to the name for the rest of the expedition. After swimming, we spotted a Kentucky Fried Chicken place, and our stomachs told us that it was time for a refueling stop.

Twelve chicken dinners were supplied in short order, and devoured in even shorter order. For simplicity, we ordered six regular and six extra crispy. One would have thought the world had come to an end when Jeff ended up with the kind he didn't want. Somehow he managed to choke it down. We almost left Randy in the rest room, but missed him just as we were driving out of the parking lot.

Bill and I had often heard about Bent's Old Fort, which is being restored by the National Park Service, just outside of LaJunta. It was a nice evening, so we drove out to the Fort. It wasn't really that spectacular yet, for there was only a small museum and some construction where the Fort will be erected. It is satisfying to see that our government is attempting to reconstruct a part of the history of the development of the west. Those must have been rough and hardy men to be able to endure the hardships of the late 1800's.

In the museum Bill was trying to listen to a recording telling about Bent's Old Fort when a small dog ambled into the room and started to lift his leg over a buffalo head that was on the floor. The kids started yelling at the dog, and Bill, not seeing the dog, started yelling at the kids to be quiet. I started laughing at both, which didn't help the situation. Our gang was in the cars ready to leave within a few minutes. Great historians our Scouts will never be!

Back at the Kiva we were joined by another crew from Overland Park, Kansas, for the night. We went for a walk around the campus of a Junior College that adjoins the Kiva grounds and prepared to hit the sack. Just after we were bedded down Buck Burshears, the adult advisor for 42 years of the Koshare Indian Dancers, came into meet us. He is a great Scouter who has given most of his life to Scouting. We asked him to tell our troop a little about the history of the Koshares, which he gladly did. He then invited Bill and me over to his home for a visit. Even though it was nearing 11:00 P.M., we accepted. His home is a museum in itself, being filled with Indian art and other articles. We finally said good-by to this great man of Scouting and returned to the Kiva about midnight, for a night's sleep.

Philmont—Day 3

This was the day we had been waiting for. Today we were to arrive at Philmont. We were up at 6:00 A.M. and downtown for breakfast at the Kit Carson Hotel when it opened at 7:00 A.M. It was an old hotel that obviously had been the hub of activity in its time before jet planes and fast automobiles. A good breakfast was enjoyed, and soon we were headed southwest across some flat and desolate Colorado countryside.

We got our first look at the Rocky Mountains just before getting to Trinidad. The atmosphere was a little too hazy for us to be able to see Pike's Peak to the north. We followed the Santa Fe Railroad up Raton Pass and pulled over to the side of the highway at the New Mexico reception center. The boys spotted an old abandoned railroad car down in the canyon and were off to investigate it.

The next stop was an old abandoned ghost town just outside of Cimarron. We were running a little late but took time for the boys to explore a couple of the old buildings. One of the boys had his picture taken while perched on the throne in an old one-hole privy that was minus its door. I was surprised that no one had burned it down in all of these years.

By then we were starting to see some familiar sights, and pointed them out to the boys as they came into view. First was the Tooth of Time, of which only the back face could be seen from our vantage point. Off to the south rising high above the valley floor was Uracca Mesa. In the distance to the west was Baldy, which we would climb toward the end of our trip. It looked very high and very far off now. Cathedral Rock could be seen straight ahead in the distance. Those familiar sights brought back many fond memories, and the anticipation of more adventure to come in the next two weeks.

Within a few minutes we had passed through Cimarron, past the "Welcome to Philmont" sign, past the Philmont air strip on the right, past the buffalo pasture (without any buffalo this particular morning) on the right, past the Villa Philmonte on the left, past the training center also on the left, and finally arrived at the entrance to tent city with the old hiking boots thrown across the gateway. The boys could stop wondering what it would be like, for now they would start experiencing Philmont first hand.

We were greeted by friendly faces as soon as we stepped out of the cars. Our Ranger, a member of the Philmont staff, was right there shaking our hands and making us feel welcome. The boys started pumping him with questions almost before they knew his name. He would be with us, helping us get accustomed to mountain life, answering questions, etc., for the next three days, or until he was confident that we could make it on our own. Before we could get our equipment unloaded another crew from the Saukee Area Council, led by Joe Miller and Al Pogge, came over to say, "Hi." They had arrived by train a day ahead of us and were just about ready to hit the trail. We felt right at home. It must have been my imagination, but to me there was a warm feeling about being back at Philmont; even the air smelled sweeter. Knowing what lay ahead of us for the next couple of days, I was completely at ease, ready to get the base camp check-in routine over, and head for the high country.

We had lunch in the new dining hall and started with the regular check-in procedure. This included a medical check, getting our crew picture taken, getting our trail equipment and food issued to us, a brief tour of the grounds, a review with the itinerary planner, and an equipment shakedown by the Ranger.

Since the Ranger knew that both Bill and I had been to Philmont before, he assumed that the crew knew what to and what not to take, which Bill and I also assumed was correct. This later proved to be a wrong assumption. We later wished that we had performed a more thorough shakedown.

Just before supper we were given a tour of the Villa Philmonte, which was the former home of Waite Phillips, the man who gave Philmont to the Boy Scouts of America. On the way back from the tour, my travelall started making a terrible noise. We suspected the worst, which included everything from a wheel bearing to a brake lining to an invasion by Martians. It was too late to get it fixed that day, so we just parked it for the night.

At supper in the dining hall, it was easy to pick the Scouts in clean uniforms who had just arrived at Philmont, from the ones who had just come in off the trail. I wondered what we would look like at the end of eleven days.

There was a leaders' meeting after supper where questions were answered, safety procedures were reviewed, etc. It was interesting to note that most of the leaders were at Philmont for the third, fourth, etc., time. One fellow was there for the eighth time. I must not be the only leader attracted by the magic magnet of Philmont.

Where had the usual afternoon rain been? There were a few drops, but that was all. You don't suppose that we were going to be in luck this year and miss all of those monsoons?

The opening night campfire told a little of the history of northeastern New Mexico, including the Philmont story, ending in a patriotic theme and the singing of "The Philmont

Hymn." It was well conducted and very impressive as a beginning to our Philmont expedition.

After the campfire we all headed for the snack bar for a last ice cream cone or soda before hitting the trail. The camp soon quieted down for everyone was anticipating the following day when we would head into the high country. There was a noticeable cool bite to the mountain night air.

Philmont—Day 4

Normal operating procedure should be for the adult advisor to have the crew leader get the rest of the crew up and moving so that the adults can sleep in until just before breakfast is ready to be served. Now if only we could have found a way to get the crew leader out of the sack, we would have had it made.

Shortly after breakfast I nursed my ailing Travelall into Cimarron to try to find a garage that could fix the noise that was getting progressively worse. There were two garages in town. One was booked solid with work, and the other was open, but the mechanic wouldn't be in for an hour. We decided to wait the hour for the mechanic. How does one kill an hour in downtown Cimarron?

Before we left for town, we strongly suggested that our crew stay together, and visit the Seton Museum and Library which was within walking distance of tent city. Knowing how much our crew loved museums, I wasn't really sure where they would be by the time we returned.

Believe it or not, the mechanic arrived on the scene right on schedule and he even looked sober for a Monday morning. He listened for a minute to the tiger in my Travelall, mumbled, got a screwdriver and flashlight, mumbled some more, poked around behind the front wheel, mumbled some more, and said, "All fixed. That'll be fifty cents, please." What a relief that was. A little rock had gotten in the brake lining somehow and was scraping. And the price was certainly right.

Driving back to Philmont, I was so startled that I almost ran into the ditch. There was our whole crew, grouped together big as life, coming out of the Seton Museum. Fantastic! A whole two hours in a museum without anyone's holding a club over them. They had found old issues of Boys' Life and had been reading the comics for years back.

We still had plenty of time to kill before our bus left for our starting camp after lunch, so we loaded the crew into my Travelall and headed south to Sayado to see the Kit Carson home and museum, which is located right on the Santa Fe Trail. There weren't any Boys' Life there, so the attention span was about ten minutes.

After lunch we all took our packs to the bus loading area and weighed them. This was the point two years ago where we discovered that our crew leader, whose pack looked the fullest, had assigned himself to carry the total supply of toilet paper. He just couldn't understand why we thought that it would be a better idea to let the little guys carry the toilet paper. My pack weighed 42 pounds, which was just about right. Most of the boys' packs ranged from 28 to 38 pounds when we started. That spread was too great, so we redistributed some of the troop equipment and food until the range was narrowed from 31 to 36 pounds for the boys.

True to form the bus was right on time, and it started to rain just as we got on board. A twenty minute ride south through Rayado, west along the Rayado Creek, and we were at our starting point. It was still spitting a few drops of rain, but not hard enough to dampen our spirits. Our Ranger gave a few minutes of map and compass instruction, and we were off.

I took the lead, and Bill Rummenie brought up drag, which was the way we would keep it most of the trip. We only had a few miles to go the first day, so I set an easy pace to allow the boys to get accustomed to the thin mountain air, get their packs adjusted, etc. The big distraction after going about a block was a giant beetle walking across the road, I only hoped that beetle would keep going on its present course and not find its way into my sleeping bag in the night.

The Rayado Creek was babbling along far below on our left. The water looked cold and clear. There were logs and debris strewn along both banks, which had washed down from the high country several years earlier during a flood. It was obvious that firewood would be plentiful.

I had studied the map the evening before and now spotted our campsite across the creek on the left. The trail would take us another half mile west to New Abreu Camp, where we could cross the stream on a one log bridge, and then double back in the canyon to Rayado River Camp where we were to spend the night.

There were several troops in ahead of us, but we located a nice spot with ample flat ground for pitching our tents. Camp was pitched with little fuss or trouble, and we still had some free time before supper. Our Ranger was having an easy time of it, for our crew obviously knew how to camp, how to cook, etc.—and it wasn't raining—yet.

The boys were introduced to a powdered concentrated soap for covering the bottom of pots before putting them on the fire. That became the dishwashers' job to soap the pots before each meal. Supper was accomplished without a catastrophe, and the dishes were completed just as it was getting dark. All in all it had been a pretty good day. Everyone wandered off to his tent shortly after dark, leaving our Ranger sleeping in Ben's hammock by the fire. I guess he stayed there all night.

Philmont—Day 5

We were up with the first light (about 5:00 A.M.) which was to be the rule for the rest of the expedition. This was to be one of our better breakfasts with powdered eggs, freeze dried ham, etc. Our crew still hadn't really gotten accustomed to the taste of the dehydrated food, nor had they been away from civilization long enough to get really hungry, so Bill, our Ranger, and I had all we could eat. That wasn't to last for long as we were soon to learn. We had camp broken and were on the trail by 8:00 A.M. That wasn't bad time, but we could do a lot better once we got it all together, and got the routine down pat. The first leg of the hike was only a few hundred yards, for we stopped at New Abreu Camp to take part in the high powered rifle instruction and shooting. There were two lounge chairs on the porch of the staff cabin. Age and rank do have their privileges. Bill and I evicted the boys from the chairs and settled in comfortably.

Most of the Philmont staff were quite friendly and overly cooperative, but here at Abreu they must have eaten a cactus or two for breakfast. Perhaps they were still suffering from the early morning grumps. They finally came out and took our crew, plus another crew from Chicago, up to the rifle range. After a brief safety instruction period, the boys were allowed to shoot the 30-06 high powered rifles. Bill and I stayed awhile, but soon decided to wait for our gang from the vantage point of the lounge chairs on the cabin porch. Most of the Scouts seemed to enjoy this program.

About 10:00 A.M. the crew was back, and then were ready for the first big test. From looking at the map I knew we had to climb over 2,000 feet in elevation and cover about five miles. The boys didn't realize what that meant just by looking at the map, but experience told Bill and me that it would take all the steam some of them could muster.

I intentionally set a fast, steady pace. If they could make the climb today, the rest of the trip would seem like fun. There were to be days when we would climb higher and travel farther, but by then they would be accustomed to the pack, the thin air, and the strenuous exercise. This day was their biggest test, but of this they were not yet aware.

Bonito Canyon was heavily wooded and steep on both sides. The trail went up and down the sides of the canyon, crossing

Bonito Creek several times. One minute would find us high above the creek, and a few minutes later we would be walking alongside the flowing water. The scenery was beautiful, but I was afraid that most of the boys were working so hard just trying to keep up that they didn't see anything.

It is so seldom that one can travel without the noise and bustle of civilization. No broken down buildings or acres of concrete in sight! No billboards or telephone poles! No automobile horns or factory whistles to break the silence! One could not help but wonder if this canyon didn't look about the same several hundred years ago. Can we really call our technology progress? Is our world really any better than that of our forefathers? There are, of course, no right answers to these questions, but it is indeed refreshing to be able to step back into history, even if just for awhile, to see unspoiled natural beauty as it was before man invaded. Only the rumble of a jet far overhead brought us back to the 1970s from the days of the early 1800 pioneer.

Our crew seemed to be doing pretty well. Randy, Jeff, and Tim were having a little trouble keeping up. They were puffing hard and their faces were a little flushed. Bill, Tom, and Ben looked fresh as a daisy after a few minutes rest. The rest of us were in varying stages of collapse. We stopped for short but frequent breaks, most of the time leaving our packs on but resting them against a tree. After an hour of climbing, I was well pleased with the pace we were setting. We had left the crew from Chicago far behind out of sight.

In another hour we came up out of the canyon into a relatively flat meadow. We had it made now. There we unshouldered our packs and took about a fifteen minute rest. There was no doubt in my mind—this crew would all make it. It was a hop, skip and jump until we were at our trail camp for the night. It was Lower Bonito Camp, which in my opinion, was one of the prettiest camps at Philmont. That night we were the only troop in camp, so had the place all to ourselves.

Since we were hungry after that long climb, and since it wasn't raining, we decided to cook our supper, and save our trail lunch for evening. That was an excellent incentive, for the crew had a fire going, the pots soaped, and supper on in short order, while Bill and I rested our weary bones, of course. Our Ranger was strumming on his guitar from his perch in Ben's hammock, which added a note of peacefulness to the setting.

Lower Bonito Camp was situated in a small, open meadow off to the south of the larger meadow through which Bonito Creek flowed. Behind our camp was a stand of tall ponderosa pines. Wooded hills rose on either side of the camp. On one end of the larger meadow was Bonito Canyon through which we had just come, and several miles on the other end was Beaubien Camp. Straight across the meadow from camp towered Trail Peak, over a thousand feet above us. Near the top of Trail Peak was the wreckage of a military plane which had crashed many years earlier. The wreckage could still be easily located and identified.

Late in the afternoon it was still clear and we were pretty well rested, so we decided to climb Trail Peak to see the plane wreckage, and to say that we had climbed our first peak. A couple members of the crew stayed in camp with our Ranger, but the rest of us took our trail lunches and plenty of water and headed west along Bonito Creek to a point where we could start up the west side of the mountain. When we got within sight of the wreckage, we let each person go at his own pace to find the rest of the wreckage. Several of us got to the seven crosses which were erected for the seven crew members who were killed in the crash.

We were still about a hundred feet in elevation and a quarter mile in distance from the top of Trail Peak. Far in the distance we could see smoke rising from campfires at Beaubien, where supper was probably being prepared by other Philmont crews. Randy and Mike still had not reached the crosses when we heard the rumble of thunder and saw lightning strike Burn Peak across the valley to the south. The top of a mountain was not the place to be during a lightning storm. We immediately headed down the mountain as fast as we believed we could safely go. Only when we were well away from the peak did we stop to put on ponchos, for it had started to sprinkle.

By the time we got down the mountain the sun was out again. We were plenty hungry by that time, so broke out the trail lunches. Both Bill and I had run low on water, so took some of Randy's which he had gotten from a creek, and to which he added an iodine tablet, earlier in the afternoon, I don't know if it was caused by the water, by running off the peak so fast, or by eating so soon after the strenuous exercise, but both Bill and I came down with a terrible stomach ache within five minutes of drinking the water. We were slow walking back to camp, but were back to normal by the next morning.

Before the day was over a few disciplinary measures were needed. Tom had to be reminded that there was Marine language used while in the Marines, and there was Scout language used while at Philmont, and he was not to confuse the two. Our crew leader had to be reminded of common courtesies that were to be shown a Philmont ranger. Fortunately neither had to be reminded a second time.

It was good to lie in the tent after everyone else had fallen asleep and know that all of our crew had met the challenge of the day and had come through with flying colors. We were on our own for the rest of the trip as our Ranger had just pulled out. He was walking back into base camp in the dark so that he could have an extra day off. I guess he knew that we were no longer in need of his assistance. All was quiet except for a breeze blowing through the pine trees at the end of the meadow.

Philmont—Day 6

I awoke to the sound of mooing cattle, not in the distance, but right outside the tent. Looking out, I saw that the campsite was full of cows just passing through. I guess we were strangers in their home. They left us several piles of souvenirs before they departed.

As usual, I was the first one up and our crew leader was last. One of our more wide awake Scouts made a mad dash down the hill frantically attempting to take pictures of the departing herd of cattle. He was snapping pictures as if they were going out of style until reminded that there were plenty of cows back home in Illinois.

Breaking camp was a terrible experience. We had only a trail breakfast to eat which required no fire and no dishes. I found a cup and spoon on a log where someone had neglected to pick them up the night before. I slipped them into my pack unnoticed. It seemed as if it took forever for some of our crew to do a simple thing like take down a tent. What had taken ten minutes the previous day took thirty this day. Finally we were headed out of camp, but with Mike falling far behind. We then tried putting him in the lead, but that was a mistake also, for he took off like his tail was on fire. Even I couldn't keep up with him. We reached a happy medium by putting him second in line, which worked great, thus we headed up Fowler Pass with the dew still on the ground, and the sun just beginning to penetrate the bottom of the valleys.

The climb over Fowler Pass was a relatively easy one. From the Pass we could see the Tooth of Time ahead on the right, Shaefer's Peak straight ahead, and Grizzly Tooth ahead slightly to the left. Down in the valley was Crater Lake Camp where we were going, to take part in their bow hunting program.

For some unknown reason we had to wait an hour before the staff was ready to put on the program. In the meantime, they gave us a couple of frisbies to pass the time. Within five minutes our smart crew had thrown them both into the lake, far out of reach. The lake was more like a small farm pond, so they undoubtedly floated back to the bank later in the day. The big pastime while waiting for the staff was watching a snake swallow a frog by the side of the lake.

It was there at Crater Lake two years before that our crew really made me proud of them. In the afternoon Jeff had twisted his ankle while running the orienteering course. Cold spring water helped it, but still it was obviously swollen. One of the staff had looked at it and indicated that Jeff would probably need to be driven back to base camp the following morning. Upon returning to camp after the coffee hour that evening, I discovered that Kirk had lashed together a pretty good makeshift crutch, and the rest of the crew had divided all of Jeff's gear so that he had only an empty pack to carry the following morning. I believe they would have carried him over Fowler Pass rather than have him taken back to base camp. At dawn the next day, Jeff, accompanied by another Scout, started hobbling up Fowler Pass, eating a trail breakfast as they went. The rest of us hurriedly broke camp and headed up the trail before the Crater Lake staff could again suggest that Jeff return to base camp. We caught up with Jeff about at the top of the pass. He was making painful, but slow progress. From the expression on his face, there was no doubt but that he was going to keep up with us. It is true teamwork like was demonstrated by our crew at Crater Lake that indeed makes a leader proud.

After the bow hunting program, we decided to eat lunch before going on to Miner's Park, our next camp. It was only after Randy was ready to mix his drink that he discovered his spoon and cup were missing. "Would someone steal a cup and spoon?" After a few anxious moments of pawing through his pack from top to bottom, the cup and spoon were presented in a fitting ceremony and another valuable lesson was learned.

On the way to Miner's Park we heard the thunder again start to roll and saw lightning flashing around Grizzly Tooth, now almost straight above us. We had the crew space out with at least fifty feet between each hiker. Our trail was in a valley, and not near any single tree, so was as safe a place to be as any. The fifty foot spacing gave us the little added protection that if there was a strike nearby, only one of the crew would be affected. Just as we came within sight of the Miner's Park staff cabin, it really started to pour. That was our first really hard downpour. We left our packs in a pack line against a tree and huddled on the porch of the cabin, along with two other crews trying to stay as dry as possible.

From our vantage point on the porch, everyone was wondering just how dry our packs oould be on the inside when the rain stopped. Most were nylon, so I wasn't very worried. They were made to take the wet weather. All Tom could talk about was to wonder if his Eddie Bauer sleeping bag, his Eddie Bauer jacket, his Eddie Bauer this, and his Eddie Bauer that would stay dry out in the rain. He became known as Eddie rather than Tom for the rest of the trip.

One of the Miner's Park staff started talking to the boys on the porch about how it was back in the days of the lumber camps. He talked about cutting railroad ties, about the old woods tools, and about the life of the lumberjack. He did an excellent job of keeping everyone's mind off the increasing rain and cold wind that had picked up. He kept our attention for about an hour, which was just about how long the rain lasted. When it did finally stop, we set up camp, and were pleasantly surprised to find that most of our equipment had stayed dry inside our packs.

At Philmont the chipmunks would find their way into packs looking for food at every opportunity. For this reason they were called mini bears. One afternoon John, who was a little on the chunky side, started growling like a real bear, thus was quickly given the name Mini Bear which also stuck for the rest of the trip.

Later in the afternoon the crew went to take part in the program which was cutting railroad ties like was done back in the days when lumbering was at its peak at Philmont. They also had a pond with several big logs in it to be used for log rolling. That looked like fun, except for falling off into the muddy pond.

When the crew came back to camp, we at first thought a black boy had come along with them to visit, but soon realized that it was Mike. How he managed to get that muddy I can only imagine. Nothing short of surgery would ever get his knees clean. He reminded us of Pig Pen in the Peanuts comic strip, and that nickname was coined for the remainder of the expedition. I believe that he actually took pride in the accomplishment of getting the dirtiest the fastest. I believe also that Mike was toying with the idea of not taking a shower until he returned to base camp, but the ultimatum of no shower— no supper, quickly sent him scurrying toward the shower house to build a fire under the wood fired boiler used to heat the water.

After supper all of the leaders in camp gathered at the staff cabin for coffee or hot chocolate, and a general bull session. When Bill and I returned to camp, most of the crew had already turned in for the night. Ben was asleep in his hammock. I hoped that no bear would make a mistake and think he was a big bag of food hanging there between two trees. One friendly swat from a curious bear could have left Ben sleeping in the vertical position for the rest of the expedition.

Philmont—Day 7

The day again started with a clear sky. Breaking camp was accomplished much smoother than the previous day. This would be our longest hike in miles, for we were going to take a side hike to the Tooth of Time; however, the side hike would be without packs. The trail up to Shaefer's Pass was not too difficult. When we got there Bill took us over to the spring where we could refill our canteens. Surprise! The spring was dry except for some stagnate water with bugs swimming around in it. After a second look we decided that we had plenty of water already in our canteens. We dropped our packs on Shaefer's Pass, took four full canteens, and headed up toward Shaefer's Peak, across Tooth Ridge, to the Tooth of Time.

It seemed as if we had gone forever. We started to wonder if we had passed it by mistake. Bill decided to bushwhack to the top of the Ridge to see if he could get his bearings. Fifteen minutes went by, and he didn't return. We started to climb to the face of the Ridge also, and soon broke out of the brush right at the back base of the Tooth. There was Bill on top of the Tooth several hundred feet above us. He later said that he called and called to us to follow him, but that we were making so much noise talking about pizzas, Big Macs, T-bone steaks, etc., that no one would answer him, so he said the heck with us and kept on climbing. After climbing over many large boulders, we made it to the top of the Tooth of Time, a familiar landmark to many New Mexico travelers.

The view was beautiful from there. We could see Crater Lake, the Stockade, Lover's Leap. Cimarron, Trail Peak, Baldy, and many other familiar landmarks. We stayed on top for about fifteen minutes before deciding to head back. It was near lunch time, and we had a long hike back to our packs on Schaefer's Pass. We soon discovered that over half of our water was gone, and the sun was really starting to beat down.

Tom was nursing the canteen having the most water. Every time anyone would start to take a swallow, one would have thought an elephant was standing on his big toe. The day before we couldn't turn the rain off, and now most of us would give a dollar a swallow. We had definitely used poor judgment regarding how much water to bring with us. We couldn't get any from the Scouts we met going the other direction, for they would need all they had to get to the Tooth and back. The shortest route to more water was to keep going to our packs.

Once we got to Shaefer's Peak, we knew it was all downhill from there. Randy and a couple of the others were really starting to drag. We finally got to our packs where we had five full canteens. What a relief, but additional water was still several miles ahead of us at Clark's Fork, our camp for the night.

If we ate lunch, we would run short of water before getting to Clark's Fork. If we didn't, we would get grouchier than we already were. We compromised and ate a candy bar, saving the rest of the lunch until we reached Clark's Fork and additional water. After a thirty minute rest, we headed down the trail for Clark's Fork, which fortunately was all downhill.

It was the first time that I had seen this trail even though it was the second time I had hiked it. On the previous trip our crew had camped at Upper Clark's Fork and wanted to hike to Shaefer's Peak in time to see the sunrise. A little mental arithmetic indicated that we would have to break camp at 2:30 A.M. in order to make it to the peak by sunrise. I assumed that no one would wake up, but was mistaken. I was amazed that everyone was up right away and working to quietly break camp. It took only thirty minutes to get everything ready and hit the trail.

It was an eerie feeling to be going up that trail in the dark of night with only the dark shadow of a mountain towering overhead on the left and nothing on the right but space and darkness. We made it to the peak before first light and stayed until after the sun poked its head over the horizon. It may not have been the smartest thing to do, but it was a memory which that crew would not soon forget.

Upon arriving at Clark's Fork we finished lunch, set up camp, I took off my dusty boots, propped my tired feet against a tree, and started to go to sleep when the inevitable happened. It started to rain. The only plan I changed was that I fell asleep inside my tent instead of leaning against a tree. When I awoke a couple of hours later, it was raining harder than ever. Then I discovered a serious mistake that I had made. In my rush to set up the tent, I had put the tent door facing uphill to the southwest; the direction from which the rain was coming. Even a novice camper knows better than to do that. The only harm done was that some of our gear got a little wet in spots.

The program for the evening was the cooking of an old fashioned chuck wagon supper by the staff. That sounded great, for there was no way we would ever have been able to get a fire started in the downpour. At 5:00 P.M. about a hundred Scouts congregated around the chuck wagon. There was one big fifteen gallon tub about half full of chocolate milk, and a giant stew pot bubbling over the fire. The rain was coming down in torrents. The roads and trails were so slick that we slid most of the way down the hill to the chuck wagon. Even with all the water, Mike's knees were still coal black.

Everyone was shivering in the wet and cold rain. To keep the weight of the packs to a minimum, none of us brought along a heavy coat. The staff dished out extra big portions of steaming hot beef stew from the giant pot. Each Troop huddled around in its own little circle, with every Scout bending over his plate to keep as much rain water as possible out of it. I had never tasted anything so good. It could have been dog meat for all I cared, as it was hot and filling. There were even seconds as long as it lasted. Needless to say, the evening campfire program was rained out. It was unfortunate, for the Clark's Fork campfire was one of the better programs at Philmont.

The leaders again gathered at the staff cabin for coffee later in the evening. This camp had showers and a laundry tub that had holes in it big enough to stick your finger through. A few boys had washed clothes and others had taken a shower. No one knew when we would ever be able to get our clothes dry. The rain had slackened a little when we were ready to walk back to our camp, but never did stop completely. It was still raining when I finally fell asleep in a slightly damp sleeping bag.

Philmont—Day 8

I awoke at the usual 5:00 A.M. to the sound of rain still falling on the nylon tent. Every drop sounded like a whole bucket full. By 5:30 A.M. I still hadn't gotten up enough nerve to venture out of the sleeping bag. Perhaps if I closed my eyes, it would all just go away. By 6:00 A.M. the rain had finally stopped, and only an occasional drop from nearby trees could be heard on the tent. On getting out of the tent, I was greeted by clear sky overhead. It was certainly a welcome sight again. It looked as though the front had moved to the east out of the mountains.

Do you remember those bottles of seam waterproofing that the kids thought were so unimportant several months ago when they unpacked their new tents? Well, this night they didn't think they were so unimportant. Our campsite looked like a disaster area. Mike's and Tim's tent had completely fallen down, obviously because the stakes weren't driven in very well, and they pulled out easily when the ground got muddy. Everybody had some wet gear. I don't think that John's stuff could have gotten much wetter had he slept in a swimming pool. In spite of the conditions, everyone seemed to be in excellent spirits. We had a trail breakfast, so didn't have to bother with trying to build a fire. I wonder how long it would have taken us!

We stuffed the soggy gear into the packs and took off for Cimarroncito Camp where we were to take part in their rock climbing program. This would be our easiest day of hiking. On the way to Cito, we passed alongside a meadow with three deer grazing. They didn't appear to be frightened by us, so Tom tried to stalk them with his camera. Had Tom been an Indian, Sitting Bull would never have been able to sneak up on General Custer. I just caught sight of two wild turkeys crossing the trail in a clearing ahead. Only a few of the crew saw the turkeys before they disappeared into the timber.

Cito was Philmont's largest mountain camp, with a Commissary, Trading Post, and heated showers. The sun was shining brightly when we arrived shortly after 9:00 A.M. We took over every tree branch, fence post, and bush in sight to spread out our clothes and sleeping bags to dry. Bill and I stayed with the equipment while the crew took part in the rock climbing program. For all of our crew, it was their first introduction to rappelling down a cliff.

All day Randy didn't look as if he was feeling too well. The symptoms of altitude sickness and homesickness are almost identical in the early stages. Since Randy had been away from home many times before, we concluded it was altitude sickness. I don't believe that he really felt normal the rest of the trip.

While waiting for our crew to finish the rock climbing program, Bill and I watched a crew that was a total disaster. Their leader was totally disabled by a blister on his foot and was awaiting a truck to take him back to base camp and to bring a staff member to take over for him. He had been recruited two weeks prior to the trip, knew nothing about Scouting, didn't have the right equipment, had never worked with the boys before the day they started the trip, and didn't really like all of this "great outdoors." He had no control over his crew. They were telling him what to do and getting away with it. He was a business executive from Philadelphia whose company sponsored an inner city troop. This had been a command performance for him. What a disaster!

Our navigator for the day was Garbage Head (Tom) whose duty was to fearlessly guide us from Cito to our camp for the night at Webster Park, less than a mile away. We all eagerly followed that flash of red hair, up past the latrine, right on a trail past some campsites, stopped and looked at the map, right past the shower, stopped and looked at the map, another right past the campfire area and into a meadow, stopped and looked at the map, over a small rise, past the latrine—yes, the same latrine the second time, stopped and looked at the map, stopped and let Mr. Rummenie look at the map, and finally followed Mr. Rummenie to Webster Park.

Randy looked as if he were about to croak, so I helped him with his pack the last few blocks. Wow, was his pack heavy! On further examination his pack looked like the magician's black hat with all kinds of good things coming out. There was a heavy air mattress, a big beach towel, enough extra clothes that he could still be smelling like a rose after eleven days, and a bar of soap big enough to wash an elephant. We couldn't find the television, but it might have been in there. No wonder he was pooped lugging all that junk over the mountains.

Like many camps, Webster Park had the open air type of box latrines, which were often situated in conspicuous places. On one occasion Jeff had been perched on such a latrine doing his morning constitutional. That particular latrine was within a few feet of the trail on Uracca Mesa. Suddenly a coed Explorer group crested the ridge. I'll leave it to your imagination how the episode ended.

Webster Park was a beautiful camp situated several hundred feet above Cimarroncito. The camp was a small, relatively flat meadow hollowed out of the side of Cimarroncito Peak. The pine covered peak towered above us to the west, and the valley through which we came, off to the southeast. This was another one of my favorite camps. But one thing worried me. We were now in the heart of bear country, and it was often said that all well fed Philmont bears eat at Webster Park. Several trees, including a big birch in the middle of the meadow, had numerous, big bear claw marks where bears had obviously tried to climb in search of food hanging in bear bags. We were going to be extra careful about hanging our bear bag this evening.

Fixing supper was typical this particular night. Our crew leader, Bill Jones, was standing in the middle of the campsite doing nothing but yelling at everyone to do everything. Greg was exclaiming to the whole world for the fortyleventh time, "I don't have to do that because it isn't my job." Tim Lubbert was nowhere to be seen. Tim McEwen was yelling at Randy to hurry up and get to work, with Randy mumbling something back from inside his tent where he was tending to numerous and unending housekeeping duties inside his pack. Jeff was asking everyone in sight where the water jug was, after tripping over it three times. Then he asked what to fill it with, then where to get it. Ben was busy as a beaver doing something, but I never figured out exactly what. Was John asleep again? Of course, Tom couldn't work or he might get his new Eddie Bauer jacket dirty. Wasn't anyone going to help Mike get supper? Somehow the meal managed all to come together in about 45 minutes.

The scene had changed from the first day. The boys looked more like a bunch of vultures waiting for something to die. The only way to keep law and order was for the cook to serve the portions and serve himself last. Adults got served first, I guess to assure us that we wouldn't get left completely out in the cold. Everyone kept an eagle eye on the cook to make sure his portion wasn't bigger than the rest. Even the peas were counted to assure an equal division. Mothers, take note. Tonight there wasn't a pea, a carrot, a noodle, not even a drop of bug juice left. If Bill and I ever let down our guard regarding trail etiquette, I feel confident that someone would end up spooned to death over a hard pea or soggy carrot cube. Tom made his usual rounds begging leftovers from everyone's plate. He did it more to maintain his reputation than anything else I am sure. The going price for hot chocolate packets was increasing each day.

Mike took a shower, but even that didn't help his knees much.

After supper, and after securing our food in a bear bag suspended high between two tall pines, we built a nice campfire in our campsite and sat around it telling of trips and adventures in days gone by. Gradually the crew one by one retired to their tents until only Bill and I were left to sit by the dying embers of our campfire. So ended another good day, with another long day on the trail ahead of us.

Philmont—Day 9

Our trip was now half completed. I hoped that the last half would be as good, and hopefully a little less rainy, than the first half. Breakfast was made and camp broken, better than on any previous day. Just when I was about to give up on this crew, they came through with flying colors.

On the way out of camp we stopped to shoot the breeze with Sy Runkel and his crew from Des Moines, who were camped nearby. They were a little shaken up. They had a bear wander into their camp around midnight. He couldn't get to their food in their bear bag, so tore apart their wood pile in disgust. When walking around camp, he tripped over a tent rope, and took a swipe at the tent, badly ripping the side. Fortunately, the boys were not injured but surely were scared.

Our whole hike this day was up and down, with never a level spot of ground. We went across Sawmill Canyon, over Ute Park

Pass, through Devil's Wash Basin, past Deer Lake Mesa, and stopped for lunch at Upper Bench Camp. We had hit a good pace and covered a lot of miles in a few hours. It looked as if we were on our way to a whole day without any rain. Had we been able to put all of our uphill climbs together, we surely would have made it to Heaven by this time.

Along the trail near Ute Park Pass the crew stopped for a break, and I walked ahead about half a mile to find a cut-off on the trail. A crew coming the other direction must have thought I looked like a priest, for they asked me to say Mass for them. I explained that that wasn't my bag, but that Father Rummenie, a tall bald-headed man, would be coming down the trail any minute. Bill never mentioned it, and neither did I, so to this day I don't know how Bill managed to talk his way out of that one.

We reached Vista Grande Camp by early afternoon. It was a dry and relatively unimpressive camp. There were few level spots in the campsite, and those that were relatively flat had rocks or roots poking up here and there. It was one of those "tie your leg to a tree and hope you don't slide over the cliff in the night" types of campsites.

There was a good view up Ute Canyon to the northwest with Baldy Mountain at the end of the Canyon. The small town of Ute Park was visible several miles below in the valley. This was one of the few camps where outside civilization could be seen. Perhaps that is why this was not my favorite campsite. The headlights of cars could be seen far below on Highway 64. Several of the boys went down to the Cimarron River in the afternoon to just mess around. They almost got lost on the patchwork of trails trying to return to camp.

Several hours of conservation work were required of Philmont crews in order to qualify for the 50-Miler patch. On several previous expeditions our crews have worked their fingers to the bone clearing trails, lugging rocks, building fireplaces, cleaning out springs, etc. Had they been told to do such tasks, one could probably have heard them squawk clear back in Quincy, but for a patch, they would do anything.

After supper we gathered together for a short non-denominational worship service. We noticed that most of the other crews in camp were doing the same thing. Later Bill and I walked around getting acquainted with other leaders.

Most of the Philmont trails were rough and narrow, with many switchbacks. Common courtesy dictated that the crew going downhill should step off the trail when meeting a crew coming uphill. Those encounters with crews on the trail were a good way to make instant friends. There was always a polite and friendly exchange of information regarding home towns, the camps and trails ahead, etc.

One thing we forgot to bring was a good set of earplugs. The same questions kept being raised day after day, by almost every member of the crew. Take, for instance, the question, "How much farther, Mr. Boeger?" Multiply it by six times a day, multiply that by ten Scouts, multiply that by eleven days, and then add the similar question, "How much farther, Mr. Rummenie?", and you end up with a pretty big number. The answer was always the same, "Look at the map!"

When do we eat? What time is it? What is the program at the next camp? Are we almost there? What day is this? Which trail meal do we eat tonight? What was the name of the place where we stayed last night? Are there showers at the next camp? Why not? What was George Washington's mother's name? Are you sure this is the right trail? I kept looking in my pack for the crystal ball, and behind every tree for that lost encyclopedia, but never found either one of them. But our crew never gave up asking. Someone must have told them that you never learn if you don't ask questions. I noticed that each day Bill would walk a little farther behind the last Scout. I don't know if it was because of all the gas being generated by that dehydrated trail food, or if it was to get away from all of those darn fool questions. Thank goodness for steep hills. Everyone was too busy gasping for air on the steep hills to ask any questions.

Tom had learned a trick that he thought the rest of us were too dumb to notice. He liked to walk near the front of the line, but would fade back immediately whenever we came to a gate so that he wouldn't have to wait and hold it open for the rest of the crew. Lazy as sin!

So ended another day at Philmont. I guess we all liked to complain a little, but I really did love the whole trip. I don't think that I would trade those high adventure expeditions for anything.

Philmont—Day 10

This was the day we were to go through Bear Canyon. We had never been there but we understood by reputation that it was a steep, hard climb all the way. It was a deep, narrow canyon with little vegetation. It gets down near freezing at night, and climbs to well over 100° by mid afternoon, when the sun's rays can reach the canyon floor. We were told to start into the canyon by 7:00 A.M. and try to be through it before 10:00 A.M.

We were up a little extra early this morning and broke camp without breakfast. We first dropped to the valley floor, then followed the Cimarron River downstream to the mouth of Bear Canyon. There we stopped for our trail breakfast. When we started into the canyon, it was just 7:00 A.M. There was already one crew ahead of us, and several more to come behind us. This was the heart of rattlesnake country. Shortly we could see the sun's light high on the canyon walls, but it still hadn't reached us on the canyon floor. We held a slow but steady pace most of the morning. At about 10:00 A.M. we dropped into Santa Claus Camp, which marked the end of Bear Canyon. It really wasn't as bad as we had been led to believe.

A brief rest and we were on our way to Head of Dean Camp where we were to spend the night. Every once in a while we would get a glimpse of Baldy through a break in the trees. Baldy was getting a little closer each day.

We had entered the North Country of Philmont. There were fewer trees but more rocks. The trees weren't as green but the rocks were rougher. There were fewer meadows but deeper canyons. Each section of Philmont had its own personality.

Head of Dean Camp had a friendly and cooperative staff. The program they presented centered around lumberjacking. There was another muddy hole for log rolling, but what appeared to be the most fun was pole climbing. The branches had been trimmed from two tall pine trees. The boys were given linemen's climbing spikes and could climb as high as their nerve would let them. They were secured from above with a safety line, thus could rappel off the pole from the top. While lying under a tree watching them take their turns, I couldn't help but wonder what percent of the boys in America had the opportunity to take part in an experience like Philmont, where boys could try their hands at countless new experiences in relative safety. I wondered what kind of world we would have if every boy could experience just two weeks at Philmont.

The program was concluded with the staff cooking a flapjack supper for all the Scouts. It was a welcome relief not having to cook our own meal for a change. They had a large trench with three fires going. Those fellows were great at making the biggest flapjacks that I ever saw. Good old Tom was near the front of the line, while Bill and I were near the back with almost a hundred Scouts in between. It had been a beautiful day until just as we were getting our flapjacks. The sun had been out when we came down for supper, so we didn't have our ponchos with us. We made a mad dash for our campsite balancing flapjacks in one hand and a cup of bug juice in the other, but didn't make it before the rain again cut loose. It lasted no more than five minutes and stopped just as we breathlessly reached our packs containing our ponchos.

The day had really gone well until we learned that some of our crew had used the woods instead of the open air latrines that were provided. I don't know if they were bashful or just plain ignorant. After a stiff reprimand, they were sent back into the woods with the shovel to take care of their mess.

Our hardest days of hiking were over, we were having no serious health problems, the programs were interesting, and we were well accustomed to the thin air and the weight of the packs. We had several sore throats in the crew, so stopped the practice of passing around the canteen whenever anyone was thirsty. I believe that the sore throats were more from the low humidity and heavy breathing than anything else. None seemed to last more than a day.

Philmont—Day 11

We were up at the usual time, even though we had a relatively easy climb to Baldy Town where we would spend two nights in the same camp. This was the last day that crews would be arriving at Philmont this summer, so the mountain population should start to thin out. One could tell that the summer was coming to an end, for many of the staff members were talking eagerly of returning to their homes.

The trail took us along the top of Baldy skyline. We had a good view of the valley on either side of the skyline. I couldn't help but think this would be a very poor trail to be on in a thunderstorm but the sky was still clear. We passed through Eell's Park Camp by mid morning and saw some troops that were just getting breakfast started.

We were in Baldy Town by late morning. We were pleased to find a trading post of sorts and heated showers. Even Baldy Town appeared to be getting a little more civilized compared with previous years. Also, the staff had the makings for peach cobbler, which we couldn't refuse, even if it did mean carrying a cast iron dutch oven back to our campsite. The campsite was in a heavy stand of young aspen trees. The ground was moist and spongy. The trees were so thick that the sun never shown into the campsite. There was no view because of the thickness of the forest. We couldn't even see other crews camped less than a block away. The smoke seemed to hang in the moist air. It was certainly a contrast to other campsites where we had previously camped. It was a good example of the varied environment that is native to Philmont. There was ample wood in the form of standing dead aspen.

In the afternoon a hot shower really felt good. It had been several days since I had enjoyed that pleasure. My last pair of halfway clean socks was broken out and put into service. After all the talk about how good the shower felt, Bill decided to try it. He just managed to get all lathered up with soap when the water pump broke down. He yelled loud enough that someone heard him and went down to the staff cabin to report the lack of water. A staff member disappeared over the hill, hopefully to try to fix the water pump. About then it again started to rain; not enough to wash the soap off Bill, but just enough to make it good and cold. After what must have seemed like a couple of centuries the water returned, and Bill started to thaw out. He wasn't in a very good mood for awhile after that.

Baldy Mountain was laced with old abandoned gold mine shafts. There were at least two within easy walking distance of our campsite, which were explored by all who weren't too lazy. All the shafts were sealed shut, but evidence of the old mine equipment was scattered over the area.

Bill and I were having coffee and hot cocoa in the staff cabin in the afternoon while dinner was being prepared back in the campsite. When we returned to camp we were pleased to find that the chores were all done, and everything was ready on time. We had that reassuring feeling that there was still hope for our crew.

Some of the other crews in camp were talking about getting up at 3:00 A.M. to climb Baldy in time to see the sunrise. I must admit that I was tempted, but with the heavy overcast the chances of a sunrise were pretty slim. Neither Bill nor I pushed the idea, and it was soon dropped.

Philmont—Day 12

We awoke to a thick fog. We were in no big hurry, so slept about an hour later than usual. After breakfast we started up the trail to Baldy. We didn't have to carry our packs, but did take water and our trail lunches. We planned to eat lunch on top of Baldy, and then descend the other side and go on to French Henry Mine before returning to our Baldy Town camp late in the afternoon.

About halfway up we saw two stray boys from another crew carving their initials on an old abandoned mine shaft timber. With all the natural beauty around, what could have been the incentive for anyone to carve his initials, thus leaving a scar for years to come?

Our Baldy Town Camp was right at the 10,000 foot elevation, and we had to ascend to 12,441 feet to reach the peak of Baldy. At about 11,800 feet, we broke out of the timber into a grassy meadow called the saddle. The fog had only partially lifted. We could see the peak about half the time when there was a break in the clouds. We were very surprised to find a herd of Hereford cattle grazing on the saddle. It still looked like a long climb to reach the summit. We could see the small village of Eagle's Nest in the valley to the west, but the fog was still pretty thick to the east of us. Each Scout ascended to the peak at his own pace. We were well above timberline, thus had no trees to break the wind. The higher elevation was obviously colder.

Scouts from previous days had erected a rock shelter to give a little protection from the wind. We all huddled together behind the rock windbreak to eat a quick, cold lunch. Jeff had carved a stake from a dead tree branch and stuck it in the rocks as a permanent monument to our ascent on Baldy. If that stick had been a little bigger, I would have been tempted to turn it into a bonfire. The fog settled in a little heavier, blocking all the view. It was unfortunate that the Scouts did not get to see the spectacular view from a mountain such as this. It is a sight once seen, never forgotten. This was Bill's third time on Baldy. It is said that a person climbs the first time because he doesn't know any better, the second time just to see if it was really as hard as he remembered it to be from the first time. The third-time climber has to be just plain crazy.

There were some very bold and brave chipmunks in the rocks. There was nothing to eat at that elevation except lunch from Scout crews like ours. We obliged and fed the hungry chipmunks. Then everyone with a camera had to get a picture of our crew huddled together trying to keep warm in the cold, damp wind.

Just as the last of the lunch was finished, we heard the distant roll of thunder. That was the warning signal to get off the mountaintop in a hurry. We headed down the side of the mountain as fast as we dared. It was steep and rocky, and several of our crew landed on their tails more than once. It was a good thing that John had a little extra padding, for I believe he slid halfway down the slope. If we were ever going to have a broken leg, this would have been the time. The storm, accompanied by thunder, lightning, rain, and hail hit just as we dropped below the timberline. We were on the far side of Baldy from our camp, thus there was nothing to do but keep going completely around the base of the mountain, a distance of several miles. The trail was going steeply down and getting slicker and slicker as the rain continued to fall. A few weeks earlier there had been snow in this gorge, but the August sun had melted it by this time.

We hiked through Copper Park Camp and on into French Henry, where a staff was waiting to present a program on gold mining. The rain stopped just as we arrived, and the sun started to peek through the clouds. For most of the rest of the day we saw the weather switch from ten minutes of sun to ten minutes of showers and back again. We all enjoyed panning for gold in the stream. Some thought they found a few flecks of gold, but none of us were optimistic enough to hire a helicopter to tote out our big nuggets. We then climbed a few hundred feet to the entrance of the Aztec Mine. The shower started again, and John discovered he had forgotten his coat at French Henry. We sent him hustling back for it.

Outside the mine shaft was a pile of tailings, the residue from building the shaft. It looked more like a pile of coal cinders. Another crew of boys were daring each other to jump from the top of the tailing pile. One tried it and found it was fun to roll to the bottom. Then their whole crew decided to try it. Within five minutes they were black from head to foot. Fortunately our crew was having more fun watching them make fools of themselves. I don't know how they would ever get clean, for there weren't any showers where they were to camp for the night. I saw John and Mike eyeing that pile of tailings like it might be fun to try, but they certainly received no encouragement from us.

Later in the afternoon, from the vantage point of my tent, it was amusing to watch Greg and Tim build a "smoke" on which to cook supper. Some say, "Where there's smoke, there's fire," but all I saw coming from that pile of wet aspen was a lot of smoke. Soon the breeze blew all the smoke right into Bill's tent. I guess he decided the only way he was going to get any rest was to help them build the fire. We had kept an axe hidden in Bill's pack, for we considered it too dangerous a tool for Scouts to use in the woods unless absolutely necessary. Splitting a few aspen logs to expose the dry heart wood got the fire going in a few minutes.

Getting supper ready was as much of a hassle this night as it had been a pleasure the night before. Just when the crew looked like they had really been able to put it all together, they fell apart.

The evening was enjoyed just sitting around our campfire, thinking we were almost finished with our trip. The thoughts were of mixed emotions. We wanted to get back to dry civilization, but on the other hand, didn't really want this expedition to come to an end.

Philmont—Day 13

The day again dawned bright and sunny. We were in no

hurry, for we had only a short downhill hike. Bill took the lead through country with which he was familiar. We dropped through Ute Meadows into Miranda Camp. Mountain Search and Rescue was the program at this camp, which would be conducted after lunch. Miranda was beautiful, with Baldy as a backdrop, and a green meadow spread out in front. The campsites were in the trees on the north side of the meadow, which extended for nearly a mile down the sloping hillside. Ute Creek babbled and gurgled alongside each campsite. What a great place to pitch a tent! We were told there was to be a marriage performed in the meadow in another week.

We proceeded on to Maxwell Camp to set up our camp. It was equally pretty, with a setting almost identical to Miranda. After lunch we returned to Miranda to take part in their program. For part of the demonstration, Randy was strapped into a Stokes Litter. They turned him over, upside down, sideways, shook him, etc., to demonstrate that a Stokes was the best way to carry an injured person over rough terrain. Our crew then tried carrying him across the clearing and back. They crossed Ute Creek with the Stokes, hesitated with Randy suspended over the cold water, but then returned him safe and dry to the demonstration area. I don't see how they were able to resist the temptation to give him a good dunking. Perhaps Bill's and my being there saved the day for Randy.

It was our best day weatherwise. The sun was out, which made it just great for lying in the meadow on a polypad wishing that you didn't have to go back to work in a few days.

After supper that evening, we invited Sy Runkel and his crew over for a closing campfire. We should have done it more often, for this kind of fellowship is always enjoyable. Sy gave a very appropriate Scoutmaster's Minute to close the campfire, and end our last full day in the high country.

Philmont—Day 14

Bill, our crew leader, and I were all of the opinion that our bus pick-up was scheduled for 11:00 A.M., thus were in no particular hurry to get moving. We left the tents up to dry in the morning sun, scoured the pots and pans, and generally put things back in good order for getting off the trail. We saw Sy and his crew pull out about 8:30 A.M. to catch a 9:00 A.M. pick-up. No hurry, for we still had two hours.

We broke camp and hiked to the turn-around where the bus was to pick us up at 10:45 A.M. 11:00 A.M. and no bus. 11:15 A.M. and still no bus. For some reason I asked to see the itinerary sheet which our crew leader always carried, and then discovered that our pick-up had been at 9:00 A.M. Thirty miles from base camp and no transportation. What to do? The only thing to do was for Bill and me to hike back to Miranda where they had a radio that could be used to request another bus for us. Bill was so mad I think you could have fried an egg on his bald head. The way he took off hiking for Miranda, I thought he was going to have a heart attack. I am still not sure just what he was mad at, for there wasn't a thing that could be done now to improve the situation.

We felt like a couple of dummies telling them we had missed our bus by two hours. They shook their heads in disbelief and radioed base camp for instructions. After a long silence, base camp agreed to send another bus out at 2:00 P.M. I guess they figured a group of flatlanders from Illinois were doing good to be only two hours late. That was better than we had expected, so headed back down to where we had left the rest of the crew. We had two hours to wait, no food left, and the clouds were starting to build in the west. We were sure that paying for the bus would deplete our pizza party money, but as it turned out, no one mentioned paying for the bus, and we didn't ask.

When we did finally get back to base camp, we saw Joe Miller and his Saukee Area Council crew just heading for Raton to catch the evening train. We didn't waste any time getting to the snack bar, for it had been nine hours since breakfast, and we were starved.

The check-in procedure was quick and easy. It didn't take me long to find the showers and clean clothes. Did those ever feel good! We were almost human beings again. The meal in the dining hall tasted great after two weeks of dehydrated trail food. I don't believe half the boys finished all their chicken. Our stomachs had shrunk so much that we were easily filled. Tom did his best to get his stretched out again.

The crews were starting to thin out as the summer drew to a close, and the staff was packing up and pulling out one by one each day. In a few more days the place would be virtually deserted.

The closing campfire was impressive with the crew flag being presented to the adult leaders by the crew leader. After that it was back to the snack bar for another taste of ice cream. I was tempted to take another shower just to make sure I remembered what it felt like. We all knew we had a long hot drive across Kansas the following day so headed for our cots in tent city fairly early.

Philmont—Day 15

We were up before first light to get packed and on our way.

We got the vehicles loaded, checked out of the tents, received our "We Made It" plaque, and were ready to pull out as soon as breakfast was over. We had a continental breakfast at 5:30 A.M. and were pulling out of the parking lot before 6:00 A.M.

We retraced the road that brought us, less than two weeks prior. We had covered a lot of ground, endured some hardships, learned a lot about each other, perhaps learned a little more about ourselves, and enjoyed a lot of good times together in the previous two weeks. Philmont and the mountains were soon only a memory as the miles of concrete disappeared behind us.

The roadside litter reminded us that we were again in civilization inhabited by the general public. It almost seemed strange to have hiked so many miles without seeing any litter, without having soda can tabs in the fire lays, without garbage floating in the streams.

Kansas was Kansas was Kansas. We didn't waste any time and perhaps even fudged a little on the speed limit as we headed east. We stopped for lunch and sightseeing in Dodge City. We found a restaurant that served the meal from a model train. The waitress put the plates on a flatcar, and ran the train down the counter. I believe we paid more for that atmosphere than for the hamburgers. The ice cream in the old ice cream parlor on Dodge's western street was great. Just about everything else was typical of a tourist trap, but at least the crew could say that they had been to Boot Hill, the Long Branch Saloon, etc.

We got to Newton, Kansas, by late afternoon, got the key to the Trinity Heights United Methodist Church, and made ourselves at home for the night. The gang was getting hungry again, so we headed for the Pizza Hut. We managed to devour $30 worth of pizza which tasted great. From there we sniffed our way to an ice cream store. Bill Jones won a free banana split and sold it to Bill and me for fifty cents. We really didn't need it, but you can be assured that none went to waste.

After that we returned to the church where we conducted our own worship service. Bill then presented each crew member with his Philmont arrowhead patch. It is a patch seldom traded, and in which most Scouts have a great deal of pride.

It was still hot, so I canvassed the town looking for some cold soda. The cars were gassed up, and we got groceries to fix a quick breakfast the next morning. Now that we were near home, we were all anxious to get there. It was so warm that half the crew slept outside the church on the driveway. A police car drove past in the night but didn't stop to investigate.

Philmont—Day 16

I awoke well before first light, and no one argued when it was suggested that we get an early start. I had it in mind that we could make it to Hardee's in Hannibal for a late lunch if we really pushed it, but Bill had his doubts. We ate rolls, juice, and cereal for breakfast, stuffed everything into the cars, and were off in record time. It was nonstop across the rest of Kansas, around Kansas City, past the new Kansas City Sports Complex, and finally my tanks were about empty, and the boys' were about full when we pulled into a gas station north of Kansas City. This would give us enough gas to get home, if necessary.

While everyone else was making a mad dash for the rest room, we got Ben to sneak the rest of the breakfast out of Mr. Rummenie's car. Innocently we finished our rest break and started across Missouri, with my travelall in the lead. I could smell those Hardee's hamburgers, so there was no slowing down for me.

At noon we were still 75 miles from Hannibal. We broke out the rest of the rolls from breakfast, waved a box of cereal out the window at the starving angels in the other car, and ate enough to last us. 1:00 P.M. and I could almost hear the hunger pangs coming from the second vehicle. We didn't dare slow down. Finally at 1:45 P.M., we rolled into Hardee's where Tom managed to stuff down $3.86 worth of junk. I'm glad that he was not riding in my Travelall the rest of the way to Quincy. Unbelievable!

It really had been a good trip. One could not help but be thankful that we had no serious injuries or illnesses. Hopefully the boys benefited from and enjoyed the trip, for I certainly did. There is no doubt at all in my mind that I will someday, the good Lord willing, again return to Philmont, in another year, with another crew, to again enjoy another Philmont experience.

Clyde Kangas

Chapter 10

The Future

Most fifteen and sixteen year olds have already learned all there is to know about just about everything. If you don't believe that, just ask one. It is just a sad fact of life that parents are the dumbest people on the face of the earth, with Scoutmasters only a little higher in the pecking order.

In spite of these handicaps to communication, the Scouting program very effectively encourages personal discussions in a one to one relationship between each Scout and the Scoutmaster, or his delegated assistant. This conversation is called the Personal Growth Agreement Conference (formerly called the Scoutmaster Conference). In a troop with thirty plus Scouts, it is so easy for a boy to be overlooked, and to be just another face in the crowd. The personal contact conveys to the individual Scout that he is important as an individual himself, with individual goals and objectives, individual problems, and an individual personality. Probably just demonstrating to the boy that you care about him as an individual is more important than anything that could be said in these conferences. They usually follow a pretty routine format, starting with putting the boy at ease by talking about something of interest to him. That is usually followed by trying to explore any problems he might be having, and by being a good listener. The session is normally concluded by trying to get the boy to set a personal goal that will require him to improve himself, usually through confidence building.

When a Scout achieves the rank of Eagle, the highest award for a boy in Scouting, I usually try to convey to him some of my personal philosophies toward life, in addition to the topics covered in the Personal Growth Agreement Conference.

I have, and am, really enjoying life. I have had few challenges that I could not meet, have very seldom been depressed or discouraged for any extended period of time, and genuinely am glad to be alive. I wish the same for all of my Scouts, and offer them the following four points which I believe have helped me over some rocky spots. Whether this advice is ever heard, I guess only time will tell, but I keep spitting it out everytime a Scout is ready for his Personal Growth Agreement Conference for the Eagle Scout Award.

1. Do your own thing. I guess it was during my senior year in college that I decided that there was no way I could or even wanted to please everyone all the time. As an individual I had certain values, certain ambitions, and certain beliefs that I wanted to accomplish; to live up to as an individual. I decided that I would have to "do my own thing" if I was going to be able to live with myself. Once in a while that meant going against the desires and wishes of friends, family, business associates, or peers. One must never forget that every morning it is yourself whom you are going to have to face in the mirror. It is your own conscience that you are going to have to live with. Know what you are doing is right and do it!

2. Don't sweat it. Many years ago there was a short article with this title, which I believe was in the *Reader's Digest*. It said that we shouldn't worry about things over which we have no control. Worry never solved any problem. If something bothers one, and it can be corrected, then take action, but don't just sit and worry about it. If the situation is beyond control, then "don't sweat it," but make the best of the situation, whatever it may be.

3. Set a goal for your life. I am sure we all have a mental picture in our minds of what that judgment day will be like. We are all going to face it sooner or later. I picture having to knock at the pearly gates, and having St. Peter ask, "Why do you think we should let you in here?" Seriously, what do you want to accomplish with your life? In your senior years, what do you want to be able to say, "Here is what I accomplished. Here is what my life stood for." We all need to set a goal now for what we really want to accomplish; for what we really believe is important in life. Then we need to make our everyday living, today and tomorrow, be a step toward reaching our ultimate goal. We only have one life to live here on earth, so let's not waste it.

4. Trust in God as a friend. A relationship with God is something that usually doesn't come as a lightning bolt but is developed over years of trying. Some boys are hesitant to talk about their religious beliefs. Some parents are also bashful about such conversations, thus their sons are completely ignorant regarding the beliefs of their parents. God is a friend who will never dessert you, and to whom you can always turn for guidance. A trust in God has brought me a more satisfying life.

I am sure that every individual would site a different list of beliefs, philosophies, sayings, or whatever, that have helped to make him the type of person that he is today. This is my list and I am not a bit bashful about sharing it with my Scouts. Did you ever wonder what the personal goals of a bank robber are and from whom he learned his beliefs? Our everyday influence on others is always either positive or negative but never neutral.

Due to job changes, I have moved a couple times in the past year. This gave me the opportunity to meet and work with many fine Scouters in other parts of our country. It also caused me to have a discontinuity in the role of Scoutmaster. This has resulted in my being "promoted" to serve Scouting in the role of Council Executive Board Member, and Chairman of the Council Camping Committee. For this honor and responsibility I am pleased. For Scouting to succeed, strong leadership from capable individuals is certainly needed at the administrative levels. Good management skills are desirable at all levels of the Scouting program. But you can be assured that come September, my wife will again be sewing the green and silver badge of the Scoutmaster back on my uniforms. It is at the level of the Scoutmaster where "the rubber meets the road"; where the aims and goals of the Scouting program will be won or lost. We need our best men serving as Scoutmasters, not sitting behind a banquet table wearing a clean suit, making an inspiring speech about the dedicated other guy who ought to serve boys.

I would like to close this book with a poem that was written by a fellow Scouter, Mr. Buck Burshears, Scoutmaster of the Koshare Indian Dancers in LaJunta, Colorado. This poem was written several years ago during the War on a night preceding the Koshare Christmas party. Buck Burshears, while trying to figure out something to say at the banquet the following night, had just learned that another of his boys, one of his Koshares, was missing in action. The result was the poem, "A Scoutmaster's Prayer," which Buck spent most of the night writing. It has served as an inspiration to me, and hopefully will to you also.

A Scoutmaster's Prayer

A little boy came knocking at my Scout room door,
An awfully little fellow just twelve and no more.
His eyes danced as he watched my gang at rowdy play.
"I would like to be a Scout," he said, "I'm 12 just yesterday."
In the weeks to come he found his place, a trim young Scout he made.
The tests he passed with eagerness, a thorough job sure paid.
The oath, the laws, the knots and flag, were taken to his heart.
A better man he was sure to be tho he'd just begun to start.
By the candle-lighted darkness I watched his round face beam
As the oath and law he pledged to keep—just like a prayer it seemed.
The years to come were happy ones as we followed the trail—
That greater men had laid for us far up where eagles sail.
I watched him grow from boy to man, the days were far too few,
To try and teach the important things that Scouting said were true.
I didn't know so long ago our nation he would defend,
I only saw a job to do, a helping hand to lend.
Now he's flying higher still with silver wings up there.
I pray to God the job I did was better than just fair.
He thanked me once for what I did so many years ago.
It was not his thanks that paid me because he did not know
That greater thanks he'd given me a thousand times before
By his dancing eyes and smiling face—could one ask for more?
There are other boys a-knocking, I must invite them in.
Please, God, give me strength to make them better men.

Biographical Sketch

Jim Boeger spent the first eighteen years of his life on a small farm overlooking the Mississippi River near Canton, Missouri. Since Scouting was not available in Canton during his early teenage years, Jim chose to be active in 4-H work. He graduated from Canton High School in 1960, received a Bachelor of Science in Mechanical Engineering from the University of Missouri at Rolla, and a Master of Science in Industrial Administration from Purdue University.

Jim and his wife Phyllis presently live in Rockford, Illinois, where he is employed with DEKALB AgResearch, Inc. Scouting honors received over the years have included Wood Badge, the Scouter's Key, Vigil Honor—Order of the Arrow, and the Silver Beaver Award. Jim is presently serving the Blackhawk Area Council as a member of the Executive Board, member of the Council Camping Committee, and Scoutmaster of Troop 425.

Clyde Kangas